Praise for *Know What You Don't Know*

"Michael Roberto has a unique knack of looking at fascinating, complex events and drawing relevant parallels in all aspects of business management. His latest book is no exception."

—**Jonathan Saxe**, Chief Information Officer—International, Morgan Stanley

"With the speed at which business can change, the ability to see around corners is paramount for business leaders. This book offers wisdom and practical ideas about how to identify (and bring to light) the most critical issues facing an organization. Leaders cannot afford to ignore his insight and advice!"

—**Paul Dominski**, former Vice President, Organizational Effectiveness, Target Corporation

"Discovering problems when they are still minor is a vital skill in today's fast-moving business environment. It is not an exaggeration to say that it is the only thing I intend to do at work every single day. This book guides you to become an 'effective problem-finder.'"

—**Shin Odake**, Chief Operating Officer, UNIQLO USA, Inc

"[This is an] insightful, useful, and richly illustrated book about the proverbial ounce of prevention—integrating stimulating case studies and a range of psychological research, Roberto's thought-provoking book shows you how to forestall crises by finding problems you didn't know existed."

—**Amar Bhide**, Lawrence D. Glaubinger Professor of Business at Columbia University, and author of *The Venturesome Economy: How Innovation Sustains Prosperity in a More Connected World*

"Michael Roberto's latest book provides an innovative and fresh approach to problem solving by focusing on problem finding. *Know What You Don't Know* offers real-world advice on becoming an effective problem hunter—on detecting the minuscule cracks before they turn into irreparable crevasses. A must-read for anyone interested in the long-term success of their project, team, or organization."

—**Scott Posner**, Executive Vice President, The Bank of New York Mellon

"Loaded with engaging examples, but also grounded in rigorous research findings, Roberto's book is a rare treat. If you want to avoid getting blind-sided as a leader, you should read *Know What You Don't Know*."

—Donald C. Hambrick, Smeal Chaired Professor of Management,
The Pennsylvania State University

"Michael Roberto has hit a home run with this book. The ability to anticipate is an essential trait to possess for any great leader of today and tomorrow. I strongly recommend this book for leaders moving from good to great."

—Joseph F. Raccuia, President and CEO,
SCA Tissue North America

"Hospitals are complex organizations where patients' lives are in our hands. *Know What You Don't Know* gave me many practical and proactive ideas to try with my leadership team to identify problems before they become catastrophes, when they can be used as opportunities for improvement."

—Constance A. Howes, President and CEO,
Women & Infants Hospital of Rhode Island

"The secret to succeeding in business is to understand that the human side of the business equation is the driver. What Michael Roberto has developed is the critical foundation to make it the reality. This is a must read!"

—John D. Callahan, former President,
Allstate Insurance

"Have you ever asked: 'How did this issue get so far?' or 'Why did we not see the early warning signs?' Wouldn't it be rewarding to know you could *prevent* problems, rather than just instituting corrective actions? Michael Roberto's fresh perspective provides practical approaches to developing problem discovery skills and capabilities. A must read!"

—Gerardine Ferlins, President and CEO,
Cirtronics Corporation

"This book describes useful techniques by which a leader can spot a problem early. It is written in an easily understandable manner, with a number of dramatic and specific examples. Professor Roberto demonstrates the global applicability of field-oriented approaches practiced by many distinguished Japanese managers."

—Shozo Hashimoto, Chairman of the Board,
Nomura School of Advanced Management

Know What You Don't Know

Know What You Don't Know

How Great Leaders Prevent Problems Before They Happen

Michael A. Roberto

Vice President, Publisher: Tim Moore
Associate Publisher and Director of Marketing: Amy Neidlinger
Wharton Editor: Steve Kobrin
Acquisitions Editor: Tim Moore
Editorial Assistant: Pamela Boland
Development Editor: Russ Hall
Operations Manager: Gina Kanouse
Digital Marketing Manager: Julie Phifer
Publicity Manager: Laura Czaja
Assistant Marketing Manager: Megan Colvin
Cover Designer: Alan Clements
Managing Editor: Kristy Hart
Project Editor: Anne Goebel
Copy Editor: Gayle Johnson
Proofreader: Paula Lowell
Indexer: Erika Millen
Compositor: Nonie Ratcliff
Manufacturing Buyer: Dan Uhrig

© 2009 by Pearson Education, Inc.
Publishing as Wharton School Publishing
Upper Saddle River, New Jersey 07458

Wharton School Publishing offers excellent discounts on this book when ordered in quantity for bulk purchases or special sales. For more information, please contact U.S. Corporate and Government Sales, 1-800-382-3419, corpsales@pearsontechgroup.com. For sales outside the U.S., please contact International Sales at international@pearson.com.

Company and product names mentioned herein are the trademarks or registered trademarks of their respective owners.

Printed in the United States of America

First Printing February 2009

ISBN-10 0-13-156815-9

ISBN-13 978-0-13-156815-0

Pearson Education LTD.
Pearson Education Australia PTY, Limited.
Pearson Education Singapore, Pte. Ltd.
Pearson Education North Asia, Ltd.
Pearson Education Canada, Ltd.
Pearson Educación de Mexico, S.A. de C.V.
Pearson Education—Japan
Pearson Education Malaysia, Pte. Ltd.

Library of Congress Cataloging-in-Publication Data

Roberto, Michael A.
  Know what you don't know : how great leaders prevent problems before they happen / Michael A. Roberto.
    p. cm.
  ISBN 0-13-156815-9 (hardback : alk. paper) 1. Problem solving. 2. Organizational change. 3. Organizational effectiveness. I. Title.
  HD30.29.R628 2009
  658.4'036—dc22
                                                                    2008033221

To my parents,
Orazio and Violante Roberto

"Ancora imparo."
—Michelangelo

Contents

Acknowledgments

When a professor writes a book, he depends a great deal on the support of the institution at which he works. The school provides the resources and the time to conduct the research. Time proves especially important for a qualitative researcher such as me, who ventures into the field often to conduct interviews and observe managers in action. I am grateful for the support of everyone at Bryant University, particularly President Ron Machtley, who asked me to join the institution two years ago. He and many others at Bryant have made me feel so very welcome. Jack Trifts, Dean of the School of Business, has been a pleasure to work with for these past two years. My faculty colleagues have engaged in many thought-provoking conversations with me. Professor Peter Nigro deserves special mention as the person who reached out and invited me to lunch on my first day at Bryant. Over time, our lunch group grew. These friends have offered good company and lively conversation, a welcome respite from my research and writing. I am also grateful to the Harvard Business School for its support, because some of the research for this book took place while I served on the faculty there.

Many people have collaborated with me on research cited in this book. I am grateful to Amy Edmondson, Jan Rivkin, Jason Park, David Ager, David Garvin, Michael Watkins, Anita Tucker, Richard Bohmer, Lynne Levesque, Erika Ferlins, and Taryn Beaudoin. Amy, Jan, and Jason deserve special mention. As a stellar young student intent on writing a great thesis, Jason joined me on dozens of interviews regarding rapid-response teams. He worked incredibly hard on the project. Jan came up with the idea of inviting Robert McNamara to speak with our students, and he worked with me on three fascinating case studies about the 9/11 tragedy and the Federal Bureau of

Investigation's efforts to reinvent itself after the attacks. As always, Amy shared keen insights with me throughout our collaborations. Amy should serve as a role model to all who aspire to conduct rigorous research that is relevant and useful to managers.

I am grateful to the many managers who spent time with me during interviews for this book, particularly all the Bryant University alumni who agreed to be interviewed. I have mentioned a few of them in the book, but many more spoke with me at length. Robert Mueller, Director of the FBI, deserves special recognition for granting us unique, extensive access to his organization during such trying times. I appreciate David Schlendorf, Sabina Menschel, and Phil Mudd's efforts to help us gain approval for the FBI research. Staff members at the Missouri Baptist Medical Center in St. Louis, St. Joseph's Hospital of Peoria, Baptist Memorial Hospital of Memphis, and the Beth Israel Deaconess Medical Center in Boston also deserve my thanks. They taught me a great deal and inspired me with their dedication to caring for their patients.

As I wrote this book, I shared many of the ideas with students in my classrooms at Bryant University, Harvard Business School, and New York University's Stern School of Business, and I refined my thinking as a result. I learned a great deal from the managers I worked with at each of my clients as well. None of those clients is mentioned in this book, because I try to keep a clear line between research and consulting. Nevertheless, the ideas benefited from extensive interaction with the managers of many companies in a wide range of industries.

I have been blessed with many wonderful teachers in my life. I certainly cannot name them all. A few of them from my youth do stand out, though—Fay Gerritt, Stephen O'Leary, Kathy Marois, Virginia Sutherland, Lou Luciani, Tom Sullivan, John McSweeney, and Jack Rose. They inspired me to become a teacher. They demonstrated that teaching truly is a vocation, not simply a job.

No book project comes to fruition without a great publishing team. I would like to express my gratitude to Tim Moore, Martha Cooley, Russ Hall, Anne Goebel, and Gayle Johnson at Wharton. They showed great patience with me as deadlines slipped on numerous occasions. Paula Sinnott, the editor on my previous book, merits recognition for persuading me to write another one.

Most importantly, I want to thank my family. They always take good care of me, especially my brother, Tony, and his family (Margaret, Nick, and Katie). My children—Celia, Grace, and Luke—kept me smiling, laughing, and generally entertained throughout this project, especially on those days when the writing became frustrating. They also showed great patience with their dad when he became a bit too "focused" on his work. My children, I love watching you grow, explore, and learn. Always keep asking good questions; let no one or nothing ever quench your thirst for learning. My wife, Kristin, makes our family go, which is a far more difficult task than writing a book. Mother Teresa once said, "Spread love everywhere you go: first of all in your own house. Give love to your children, to your wife or husband, to a next-door neighbor...Let no one ever come to you without leaving better and happier." Kristin, you embody those sentiments beautifully. Finally, I dedicate this book to my parents. From the Italian province of Avellino, they came to America in search of a better life for their children. They certainly accomplished their goal. My folks instilled in us the value of an education, and they demonstrated what it means to have a strong work ethic. I am so proud to be their son.

About the Author

Michael A. Roberto is Trustee Professor of Management at Bryant University in Smithfield, RI, where he teaches leadership, managerial decision-making, and business strategy. He joined Bryant's tenured faculty after serving for six years on the faculty at Harvard Business School. He also has been a Visiting Associate Professor of Management at New York University's Stern School of Business.

Dr. Roberto's research focuses on strategic decision-making processes and senior management teams. He also has studied why catastrophic group or organizational failures happen, including the Columbia Space Shuttle accident and the 1996 Mount Everest tragedy. His research has been published in the *Harvard Business Review*, *California Management Review*, *MIT Sloan Management Review*, *The Leadership Quarterly*, *Group and Organization Management*, and *Ivey Business Journal*. His book, *Why Great Leaders Don't Take Yes for an Answer* (Wharton), was named one of the year's top 10 business books by *The Globe and Mail*, Canada's largest daily newspaper.

Dr. Roberto has taught in the leadership development programs and consulted at Apple, Target, Morgan Stanley, Coca-Cola, Wal-Mart, Mars, Novartis, Federal Express, The Home Depot, Johnson & Johnson, Bank of New York Mellon, Royal Caribbean Cruises, and other leading firms. He has also presented at government organizations including the FBI, NASA, EPA, and TSA. Over the past five summers, he has served on the faculty of Tokyo's Nomura School of Advanced Management executive education program.

Dr. Roberto resides in Holliston, Massachusetts with his wife, Kristin, and his three children—Grace, Celia, and Luke.

Preface

In the spring of 2005, former Secretary of Defense Robert McNamara came to speak to my students. At the time, I served on the faculty at Harvard Business School. My colleague Jan Rivkin and I invited McNamara to answer our MBA students' questions about his years in the Defense Department as well as his time at Ford Motor Company and the World Bank. My students had studied the Bay of Pigs fiasco, the Cuban Missile Crisis, and the Vietnam War. We examined those case studies as part of a course focused on how to improve managerial decision-making. Most class sessions focused on typical business case studies, but students found these examples from the American presidency to be particularly fascinating. We had analyzed the decision-making processes employed by Presidents Kennedy and Johnson and their senior advisers. Now, we had an opportunity to hear directly from one of the key players during these momentous events of the 1960s. McNamara came and answered the students' questions, which included some tough queries regarding the mistakes that were made during the Vietnam War as well as the Bay of Pigs debacle.

McNamara had not visited the Harvard Business School in many years. However, he recalled his days at the school quite fondly. McNamara graduated from the MBA program in 1939 and returned a year later to join the faculty at just twenty-four years of age. The students expressed amazement that he had been on the faculty sixty-five years prior to his visit that day in the spring of 2005.

Before the class session began, McNamara asked me about my research. I told him about a new book I had written, set to come out two months later, regarding the way leaders make decisions. Then McNamara asked about teaching at the school, inquiring as to whether we still employed the case method of instruction. When I indicated that the case method still reigned supreme in our classrooms, he expressed his approval. He recalled how much he enjoyed learning and teaching by the case method. McNamara then affirmed a long-standing belief about this experiential learning technique. He explained that the case method provided students good training in the subject matter I researched and taught—namely, problem-solving and decision-making. After all, most cases put students in the shoes of a business executive and make them grapple with a difficult decision facing the firm.

McNamara then surprised me when he mentioned that this approach to teaching and learning did have a major deficiency. He argued that the case method typically presents the problem to the student. It describes the situation facing a firm and then frames the decision that must be made. In real life, according to McNamara, the leader first must discover the problem. He or she must figure out what problem needs to be solved before beginning to make decisions. McNamara explained that identifying the true problem facing an organization often proved to be the most difficult challenge that leaders face. In many instances leaders do not spot a threat until far too late. At times, leaders set out to solve the wrong problem.

Now here I stood, quite pleased that I had just completed my first book on the subject of decision-making. I anticipated its release in just a matter of weeks. I had built a solid course on the subject as well. McNamara seemed to be telling me that I had missed the boat! I needed to be helping managers and students learn how to find problems, rather than focusing so much attention on problem-solving. I wrestled with this thought over the next six months, and then in the winter of 2006, I set out to write a new book. This time, I would write about the process of problem-finding, rather than problem-solving and decision-making. Two and a half years later, I have completed that book.

The Central Message

In this book, I argue that leaders at all levels must hone their skills as problem-finders. In so doing, they can preempt the threats that could lead to disaster for their organizations. Keep in mind that organizational breakdowns and collapses do not occur in a flash; they evolve over time. They begin with a series of small problems, a chain of errors that often stretches back many months or even years. As time passes, the small problems balloon into larger ones. Mistakes tend to compound over time; one small error triggers another. Once set in motion, the chain of events can be stopped. However, the more time that passes, and the more momentum that builds, once-seemingly minor issues can spiral out of control.

Many leaders at all levels tell their people that they hate surprises. They encourage their people to tell them the bad news, rather than providing only a rosy picture of the business. They hold town-hall meetings with their employees, tour various company locations, and remind everyone that their door is always open. Still, problems often remain concealed in organizations for many reasons. Unlike cream, bad news does not tend to rise to the top.

In this book, I argue that leaders need to become hunters who venture out in search of the problems that might lead to disaster for their firms. They cannot wait for the problems to come to them. Time becomes the critical factor. The sooner leaders can identify and surface problems, the more likely they can prevent a major catastrophe. If leaders spot the threats early, they have more time to take corrective action. They can interrupt a chain of events before it spirals out of control.

Through my research, I have identified seven sets of skills and capabilities that leaders must master if they want to become effective problem-finders. First, you must recognize that people around you filter information, often with good intentions. They hope to conserve your precious time. Sometimes, though, they filter out the bad news.

Problem-finders learn how to circumvent these filters. Second, you must learn to behave like an anthropologist who observes groups of people in natural settings. You cannot simply ask people questions; you must watch how they behave. After all, people often say one thing and do another. Third, the most effective problem-finders become adept at searching for and identifying patterns. They learn how to mine past experience, both personal and organizational, so that they can recognize problems more quickly. Fourth, you must refine your ability to "connect the dots" among seemingly disparate pieces of information. Threats do not come to us in neat little packages. They often remain maddeningly diffuse. Only by putting together many small bits of information can we spot the problem facing the organization. Fifth, effective problem-finders learn how to encourage people to take risks and learn from their mistakes. They recognize that some failures can be quite useful, because they provide opportunities for learning and improvement. You must distinguish between excusable and inexcusable mistakes, though, lest you erode accountability in the organization. Sixth, you must refine your own and your organization's communication skills. You have to train people how to speak up more effectively and teach leaders at all levels how to respond appropriately to someone who surfaces a concern, points out a problem, or challenges the conventional wisdom. Finally, the best problem-finders become like great coaches who watch film of past performances and glean important lessons about their team's problems as well as those of their principal rivals. You must become adept at review and reflection, as well as how to practice new behaviors effectively.

The outline of this book is straightforward. The book begins with a chapter describing the overall concept of problem-finding. Why is it important, and what does it mean? Then, each of the following seven chapters describes one of the critical problem-finding skills and capabilities I have identified in my research. Throughout the text, I refer to the endnotes, which provide information if you're interested in learning more about the academic research upon which I have drawn.

Finally, the book closes with a chapter that examines the mindset of the problem-finder. I argue that becoming an effective problem-finder requires more than mastering a set of skills. You have to embrace a different attitude and mindset about work and the world around you. The best problem-finders demonstrate intellectual curiosity, embrace systemic thinking, and exhibit a healthy dose of paranoia.

The Research

The research for this book consisted of nearly one hundred fifty interviews with managers of enterprises large and small. I asked them to speak with me about their successes and failures and to describe how they tried to prevent failures from taking place. The interviews took place in a wide range of industries. I spoke with many CEOs as well as business unit leaders and staff executives. The field notes from these interviews, as well as other artifacts collected during my visits to these firms, filled several large drawers of the file cabinet in my university office.

Throughout the research, I sought breadth as well as depth. I conducted single interviews at a wide range of firms in many industries. I have not limited my research to private-sector enterprises; I have drawn upon many nonbusiness case studies in my work. In a few instances, I examined a particular organization in great detail. For instance, at the FBI, Jan Rivkin and I conducted many interviews with people at all levels of the bureau. For the rapid-response team study, Jason Park and I interviewed roughly twelve people at each hospital. We also observed many weekly meetings at one of those organizations. At Children's Hospital in Minneapolis, Amy Edmondson, Anita Tucker, and I interviewed a number of physicians, nurses, and administrators. At GameWright, a children's game company in Massachusetts, Taryn Beaudoin and I spent a great deal of time learning about the organization and interviewing managers.

I have sought to conduct research that is fundamentally interdisciplinary in nature. Throughout my field studies, as well as my review of others' work, I have drawn upon the literature in domains as diverse as psychology, political science, marketing, sociology, economics, neuroscience, and medicine. No one field has a monopoly on issues pertaining to leadership. I have conducted research, and drawn upon others' work, that I believe is highly relevant to the practice of management. Far too much research conducted at business schools today has little or no value to business leaders. While I cite a number of important experimental studies throughout the book, I have tended to emphasize the findings from intensive field research where other scholars and I have spoken with and observed real managers in action.

How to Read This Book

You probably have significant demands on your time. For this book to have value, you must be able to apply the ideas to your work. You must come away with tangible changes in how you go about leading your teams and organizations. Therefore, I encourage you to adopt an active learning approach as you read this book. Do not simply turn the pages and try to digest the ideas. Simply reading the text represents passive learning, which typically has less impact than a more engaged approach. As you examine the manuscript, begin to think about how to put the ideas into practice. Try implementing some of the concepts in your organization. Bounce your ideas off valued colleagues. Do not wait until you finish the manuscript. Experiment with the ideas presented here, reflect on your experiences, and refine your approach. Try to make the ideas come alive for you. Find the techniques that best fit your style of leadership and the demands of your organization.

Finally, keep in mind that becoming a better leader is a never-ending journey. No book can provide a recipe for transforming you into a successful leader. It will not happen overnight. Even the best leaders have opportunities to improve. I can only hope that this manuscript stimulates you to think differently about your roles and responsibilities as a leader. Perhaps you will take a fresh look at how you and your colleagues approach problems and mistakes. If you avoid a major failure in part because of what you have learned here, this book will have served a very useful purpose.

Michael A. Roberto
Smithfield, Rhode Island
July 23, 2008

1

From Problem-Solving to Problem-Finding

"It isn't that they can't see the solution. It's that they can't see the problem."

—G. K. Chesterton

Code blue! Code blue! Mary's heart has stopped, and her nurse has called for help. A team rushes to the patient's room. No one expected this crisis. Mary had come to the hospital for routine knee-replacement surgery, and she had been in fairly good health prior to the procedure. Now, she isn't breathing. Working from a "crash cart" full of key equipment and supplies, the expert team begins trying to resuscitate the patient. Working at lightning speed, yet with incredible calm and precision, they get Mary's heart beating again. They move her to the intensive care unit (ICU), where she remains for two weeks. In total, she spends one month more than expected in the hospital after her surgery. Her recovery, even after she returns home, is much slower than she anticipated. Still, Mary proved rather lucky, because the survival rate after a code blue typically does not exceed 15%.

After Mary begins breathing regularly again, the patient's family praises the team that saved her life. Everyone expresses relief that the team responded so quickly and effectively. Then, the team members return to their normal work in various areas of the hospital. Mary's nurse attends to her other patients. However, as she goes about her

normal work, she wonders: Could this cardiac arrest have been fore-
seen? Did I miss the warning signs? She recalls noticing that Mary's
speech and breathing had become slightly labored roughly six hours
before the arrest. She checked her vitals. While her respiratory rate
had declined a bit, her other vital signs—blood pressure, heart rate,
oxygen saturation, and body temperature—remained normal. Two
hours later, the nurse noticed that Mary appeared a bit uncomfortable. She asked her how she was feeling, and Mary responded, "I'm
OK. I'm just a little more tired than usual." Mary's oxygen saturation
had dipped slightly, but otherwise, her vitals remained unchanged.
The nurse considered calling Mary's doctor, but she didn't feel comfortable calling a physician without more tangible evidence of an
urgent problem. She didn't want to issue a false alarm, and she knew
that a physician's assistant would come by in approximately one hour
to check on each patient in the unit.[1]

This scenario, unfortunately, has transpired in many hospitals
over the years. Research shows that hospitalized patients often dis-
play subtle—and not-so-subtle—warning signs six to eight hours
before a cardiac arrest. During this time, small problems begin to
arise, such as changes in heart rate, blood pressure, and mental status. However, hospital personnel do not necessarily notice the symptoms. If they notice a problem, they often try to address it on their
own, rather than bringing their concerns to the attention of others.
One study found that two-thirds of patients exhibited warning signs,
such as an abnormally high or low heart rate, within six hours of a cardiac arrest, yet nurses and other staff members brought these problems to the attention of a doctor in only 25% of those situations.[2] In
short, staff members wait too long to bring these small problems to
the attention of others. Meanwhile, the patient's health continues to
deteriorate during this window of opportunity when an intervention
could perhaps prevent a crisis.

Several years ago, Australian hospitals set out to save lives by acting sooner to head off emerging crises. They devised a mechanism

whereby caregivers could intervene more quickly to address the small problems that typically portend larger troubles. The hospitals invented Rapid Response Teams (RRTs). These teams respond to calls for assistance, typically from a floor nurse who notices an early warning sign associated with cardiac arrest. The team typically consists of an experienced critical-care nurse and a respiratory therapist; in some cases, it also includes a physician and/or physician's assistant. When the nurse pages an RRT, the team arrives at the patient's bedside within a few minutes and begins its diagnosis and possible intervention. These teams quickly assess whether a particular warning sign merits further testing or treatment to prevent a cardiac arrest.

To help the nurses and other staff members spot problems in advance of a crisis, the hospitals created a list of the "triggers" that may foreshadow a cardiac arrest and posted them in all the units. Researchers identified these triggers by examining many past cases of cardiac arrest. Most triggers involved a quantitative variable such as the patient's heart rate. For instance, many hospitals instructed staff members that the RRT should be summoned if a patient's heart rate fell below 40 beats per minute or rose above 130 beats per minute. However, hospitals found that nurses often noticed trouble even before vital signs began to deteriorate. Thus, they empowered nurses to call an RRT if they felt concerned or worried about a patient, even if the vital signs appeared relatively normal.[3]

The invention of RRTs yielded remarkable results in Australia. The innovation soon spread to the United States. Early adopters included four sites at which my colleagues (Jason Park, Amy Edmondson, and David Ager) and I conducted research: Baptist Memorial Hospital in Memphis, St. Joseph's Hospital in Peoria, Missouri Baptist Medical Center in St. Louis, and Beth Israel Deaconess Medical Center in Boston. Nurses reported to us that they felt much more comfortable calling for assistance, especially given that the RRTs were trained not to criticize or punish anyone for a "false alarm." As one said to us, "It's about the permission the nurses have to call now that they didn't have before the RRT process was established." Another nurse commented, "There is nothing better than knowing you can call an RRT when a patient is going bad." With the implementation of this proactive process for spotting problems, each of these pioneering hospitals reported substantial declines in cardiac arrests, transfers to the intensive care unit, and deaths. A physician explained why RRTs proved successful: "The key to this process is time. The sooner you identify a problem, the more likely you are to avert a dangerous situation."

Academic research confirms the effectiveness of RRTs. For instance, a recent Stanford study, published in the *Journal of the American Medical Association*, found a 71% reduction in "code blue" incidences and an 18% reduction in mortality rate after implementation of an RRT in a pediatric hospital.[4] With these kinds of promising results, the innovation has spread like wildfire. The Institute for Healthcare Improvement has championed the idea. Now, more than 1,600 hospitals around the country have implemented the RRT model. Many lives have been saved.

What is the moral of this remarkable story? Small problems often precede catastrophes. In fact, most large-scale failures result from a series of small errors and failures, rather than a single root cause. These small problems often cascade to create a catastrophe. Accident investigators in fields such as commercial aviation, the military, and medicine have shown that a *chain of events and errors* typically leads to a particular disaster.[5] Thus, minor failures may signal big trouble ahead; treated appropriately, they can serve as early warning signs. Many large-scale failures have long incubation periods, meaning that managers have ample time to intervene when small problems arise, thereby avoiding a catastrophic outcome.[6] Yet these small problems often do not surface. They occur at the local level but remain invisible to the broader organization. These hospitals used to expend enormous resources trying to save lives after a catastrophe. They engaged in heroic efforts to resuscitate patients after a cardiac arrest. Now, they have devised a mechanism for spotting and surfacing small problems before they escalate to create a catastrophic outcome. Code Blue Teams are in the business of fighting fires. The Rapid Response Team process is all about detecting smoke (see Figure 1.1).[7]

This book uses the terms *problem* and *failure* interchangeably; they are defined as a condition in which the expected outcome has not been achieved. In other words, we do not witness desired positive results, or we experience negative results. These problems may entail breakdowns of a technical, cognitive, and/or interpersonal nature. Technical problems consist of breakdowns in the functioning of equipment, technology, natural systems, and the like. Cognitive problems entail judgment or analytical errors on the part of individuals or groups. Interpersonal problems involve breakdowns in communication, information transfer, knowledge sharing, and conflict resolution.[8]

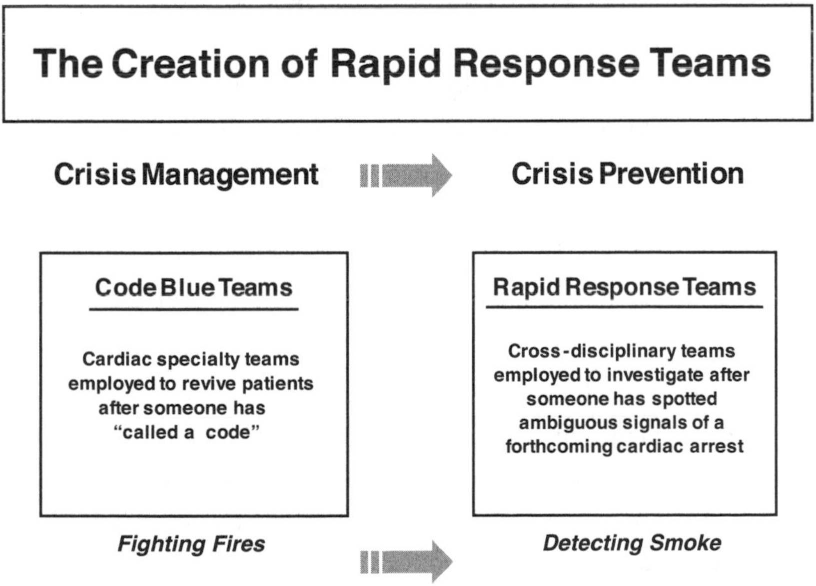

The Creation of Rapid Response Teams

Crisis Management ▮▮▶ Crisis Prevention

Code Blue Teams	Rapid Response Teams
Cardiac specialty teams employed to revive patients after someone has "called a code"	Cross-disciplinary teams employed to investigate after someone has spotted ambiguous signals of a forthcoming cardiac arrest

Fighting Fires   ▮▮▶   *Detecting Smoke*

Figure 1.1   Fighting fires versus detecting smoke

Many organizations devote a great deal of attention to improving the problem-solving capabilities of employees at all levels. Do they spend as much time thinking about how to discover problems before they mushroom into large-scale failures? One cannot solve a problem that remains invisible—unidentified and undisclosed. Unfortunately, for a variety of reasons, problems remain hidden in organizations for far too long. We must find a problem before it can be addressed appropriately. Great leaders do not simply know how to solve problems. They know how to find them. They can detect smoke, rather than simply trying to fight raging fires. This book aims to help leaders at all levels become more effective problem-finders.

Embrace Problems

Most individuals and organizations do not view problems in a positive light. They perceive problems as abnormal conditions, as situations that one must avoid at all costs. After all, fewer problems mean a greater likelihood of achieving the organization's goals and objectives. Most managers do not enjoy discussing problems, and they certainly do not cherish the opportunity to disclose problems in their own units. They worry that others will view them as incompetent for allowing the problem to occur, or incapable of resolving the problem on their own. In short, many people hold the view that the best managers do not share their problems with others; they solve them quietly and efficiently. When it comes to small failures in their units, most managers believe first and foremost in the practice of discretion.

Some organizations, however, perceive problems quite differently. They view small failures as quite ordinary and normal. They recognize that problems happen, even in very successful organizations, despite the best managerial talent and most sophisticated management techniques. These organizations actually *embrace* problems. Toyota Motor Corporation exemplifies this very different attitude toward the small failures that occur every day in most companies.

Toyota views problems as *opportunities to learn and improve*. Thus, it seeks out problems, rather than sweeping them under the rug.[9]

Toyota also does not treat small problems in isolation; it always tries to connect them to the bigger picture. Toyota asks: Is this small failure symptomatic of a larger problem? Do we have a systemic failure here?[10] In this way, Toyota resembles organizations such as nuclear power plants and U.S. Navy aircraft carriers—entities that operate quite reliably in a high-risk environment. Scholars Karl Weick and Kathleen Sutcliffe point out that those organizations have a unique view of small problems:

> "They tend to view any failure, no matter how small, as a window on the system as a whole. They view any lapse as a signal of possible weakness in other portions of the system. This is a very different approach from most organizations, which tend to localize failures and view them as specific, independent problems... [They act] as though there is no such thing as a confined failure and suspect, instead, that the causal chains that produced the failure are long and wind deep inside the system."[11]

With this type of approach, Toyota maintained a stellar reputation for quality in the automobile industry for many years. Experts attributed it to the vaunted Toyota Production System, with its emphasis on continuous improvement. As many people now know, Toyota empowers each frontline worker to "pull the Andon cord" if they see a problem, thereby alerting a supervisor of a potential product defect or process breakdown. If the problem cannot be solved in a timely manner, this process actually leads to a stoppage of the assembly line. This system essentially empowered everyone in a Toyota manufacturing plant to become a problem-finder. Quality soared as Toyota detected problems far earlier in the manufacturing process than other automakers typically did.[12] Like the hospitals that deployed Rapid Response Teams, Toyota discovered that the likelihood of a serious failure increases dramatically if one reduces the time gap between problem detection and problem occurrence. Both the hospitals and Toyota learned that acting early to address a small potential problem may lead to some false alarms, but it proves far less costly than trying to resolve problems that have mushroomed over time.

This attitude about problems permeates the organization, and it does not confine itself to quality problems on the production line. It applies to senior management and strategic issues as well. In a 2006 *Fast Company* article, an American executive describes how he learned that Toyota did not operate like the typical organization. He reported attending a senior management meeting soon after his hire at Toyota's Georgetown, Kentucky plant in the 1990s. As he began reporting on several successful initiatives taking place in his unit, the chief executive interrupted him. He said, "Jim-san. We all *know* you are a good manager. Otherwise, we would not have hired you. But please talk to us about your problems so we can work on them together."[13]

More recently, though, Toyota's quality has slipped by some measures. In a recent interview with *Harvard Business Review*, Toyota CEO Katsuaki Watanabe addressed this issue, noting that the firm's explosive growth may have strained its production system. His answer speaks volumes about the company's attitude toward problems:

> "I realize that our system may be overstretched. We must make that issue visible. Hidden problems are the ones that become serious threats eventually. If problems are revealed for everybody to see, I will feel reassured. Because once problems have been visualized, even if our people didn't notice them earlier, they will rack their brains to find solutions to them."[14]

Most executives would not be so candid about the shortcomings of the organization they lead. In contrast, Watanabe told the magazine that he felt a responsibility to "surface problems" in the organization. By speaking candidly about Toyota's recent quality troubles, rather than trying to minimize or downplay them, Watanabe models the attitude that he wants all managers at the firm to embrace. For

Watanabe and the Toyota organization he leads, problems are not the enemy; hidden problems are.

Why Problems Hide

Problems remain hidden in organizations for a number of reasons. First, people fear being marginalized or punished for speaking up in many firms, particularly for admitting that they might have made a mistake or contributed to a failure. Second, structural complexity in organizations may serve like dense "tree cover" in a forest, which makes it difficult for sunlight to reach the ground. Multiple layers, confusing reporting relationships, convoluted matrix structures, and the like all make it hard for messages to make their way to key leaders. Even if the messages do make their way through the dense forest, they may become watered down, misinterpreted, or mutated along the way. Third, the existence and power of key gatekeepers may insulate leaders from hearing bad news, even if the filtering of information takes place with the best of intentions. Fourth, an overemphasis on formal analysis and an underappreciation of intuitive reasoning may cause problems to remain hidden for far too long. Finally, many organizations do not train employees in how to spot problems. Issues surface more quickly if people have been taught how to hunt for potential problems, what cues they should attend to as they do their jobs, and how to communicate their concerns to others.

Cultures of Fear

Maxine Clark founded and continues to serve as chief executive of Build-a-Bear Workshop, a company that aims to "bring the teddy bear to life" for children and families. Clark's firm does so by enabling children to create customized and personalized teddy bears in its stores. Kids choose what type of bear they want. Store associates stuff, stitch, and fluff the bears for the children, and then the kids choose precisely how they want to dress and accessorize the teddy bear. If you have young children or grandchildren, you surely have heard of Clark's firm.

Clark has built an incredibly successful company, growing it to over $350 million in sales over the past decade. She has done so by delivering a world-class customer experience in her stores. Clark credits her store associates, who constantly find ways to innovate and improve. How do the associates do it? For starters, they tend not to fear admitting a mistake or surfacing a problem. Clark's attitude toward mistakes explains her associates' behavior. She does not punish people for making an error or bringing a problem to light; she encourages it.

Clark credits her first-grade teacher, Mrs. Grace, for instilling this attitude toward mistakes in her long ago. As many elementary school teachers do, Mrs. Grace graded papers using a red pencil. However, unlike most of her colleagues, Mrs. Grace gave out a rather unorthodox award at the end of each week. She awarded a red pencil prize to the student who had made the most mistakes! Why? Mrs. Grace wanted her students engaged in the class discussion, trying to answer every question, no matter how challenging. As Clark writes, "She didn't want the fear of being wrong to keep us from taking chances. Her only rule was that we couldn't be rewarded for making the same mistake twice."[15]

Clark has applied her first-grade teacher's approach at Build-a-Bear by creating a Red Pencil Award. She gives this prize to people who have made a mistake but who have discovered a better way of doing business as a result of reflecting on and learning from that mistake. Clark has it right when she says that managers should encourage their people to "experiment freely, and view every so-called mistake as one step closer to getting things just right."[16] Of course, her first-grade teacher had it right as well when she stressed that people would be held accountable if they made the same mistake repeatedly. Failing to learn constitutes the bad behavior that managers should deem unacceptable. Clark makes that point clear to her associates.[17]

Many organizations exhibit a climate in which people do not feel comfortable speaking up when they spot a problem, or perhaps have made a mistake themselves. These firms certainly do not offer Red Pencil Awards. My colleague Amy Edmondson points out that such firms lack psychological safety, meaning that individuals share a belief that the climate is not safe for interpersonal risk-taking. Those risks include the danger of being perceived as a trouble-maker, or of being seen as ignorant or incompetent. In an environment of low psychological safety, people believe that others will rebuke, marginalize, or penalize them for speaking up or for challenging prevailing opinion; people fear the repercussions of admitting a mistake or pointing out a problem.[18] In some cases, Edmondson finds that frontline employees do take action when they see a problem in such "unsafe" environments. However, they tend to apply a Band-Aid at the local level, rather than raising the issue for a broader discussion of what systemic problems need to be addressed. Such Band-Aids can do more harm than good in the long run.[19] Leaders at all levels harm psychological safety when they establish hierarchical communication protocols, make status differences among employees highly salient, and fail to admit their own errors. At Build-a-Bear, Maxine Clark's Red Pencil Award serves to enhance psychological safety, and in so doing, helps ensure that most problems and errors do not remain hidden for lengthy periods of time.

Organizational Complexity

In the start-up stage, most companies have very simple, flat organizational structures. As many firms grow, their structures become more complex and hierarchical. To some extent, such increased complexity must characterize larger organizations. Without appropriate structures and systems, a firm cannot continue to execute its strategy as it grows revenue. However, for too many firms, the organizational structure becomes unwieldy over time. The organization charts become quite messy with dotted-line reporting relationships, matrix structures, cross-functional teams, ad hoc committees, and the like. People find it difficult to navigate the bureaucratic maze even to get simple things accomplished. Individuals cannot determine precisely where decision rights reside on particular issues.[20]

Amidst this maze of structures and systems, key messages get derailed or lost. Information does not flow effectively either vertically or horizontally across the organization. Vertically, key messages become garbled or squashed as they ascend the hierarchy. Horizontally, smooth handoffs of information between organizational units do not take place. Critical information falls through the cracks.

The 9/11 tragedy demonstrates how a complex organizational structure can mask problems.[21] Prior to the attacks, a labyrinth of agencies and organizations worked to combat terrorism against the U.S. These included the Central Intelligence Agency, the Federal Bureau of Investigation, the Federal Aviation Administration, and multiple units within the Departments of State and Defense. Various individuals within the federal government discovered or received information pertaining to the attacks in the days and months leading up to September 11, 2001. However, some critical information never rose to the attention of senior officials. In other cases, information did not pass from one agency to another, or the proper integration of disparate information did not take place. Individuals did not always recognize who to contact to request critical information, or who they should inform about something they had learned. On occasion, officials downplayed the concerns of lower-level officials, who in turn did not know where else to go to express their unease. Put simply, the right information never made it into the right hands at the right time. The dizzying complexity of the organizational structures and systems within the federal government bears some responsibility. The 9/11 Commission concluded:

"Information was not shared, sometimes inadvertently or because of legal misunderstandings. Analysis was not pooled. Effective operations were not launched. Often the handoffs of information were lost across the divide separating the foreign and domestic agencies of the government. However the specific problems are labeled, we believe they are symptoms of the government's broader inability to adapt how it manages problems to the new challenges of the twenty-first century. The agencies are like a set of specialists in a hospital, each ordering tests, looking for symptoms, and prescribing medications. What is missing is the attending physician who makes sure they work as a team."[22]

Gatekeepers

Each organization tends to have its gatekeepers, who control the flow of information and people into and out of certain executives' offices. Sometimes, these individuals serve in formal roles that explicitly require them to act as gatekeepers. In other instances, the gatekeepers operate without formal authority but with significant informal influence. Many CEOs have a chief of staff who serves as a gatekeeper. Most recent American presidents have had one as well. These individuals may serve a useful role. After all, someone has to ensure that the chief executive uses his or her time wisely. Moreover, the president has to protect against information overload. The chief executive can easily get buried in reports and data. If no one guards his schedule, the executive could find himself bogged down in meetings that are unproductive, or at which he is not truly needed.[23] Former President Gerald Ford commented on the usefulness of having someone in this gatekeeper function:

"I started out in effect not having an effective Chief of Staff and it didn't work. So anybody who doesn't have one and tries to run the responsibilities of the White House, I think, is putting too big a burden on the President himself. You need a filter, a person that you have total confidence in who works so closely with you that, in effect, is almost an alter ego. I just can't imagine a President not having an effective Chief of Staff."[24]

Trouble arises when the gatekeeper intentionally distorts the flow of information. Put simply, the gatekeeper function bestows a great deal of power on an individual. Some individuals, unfortunately, choose to abuse that power to advance their agendas. In their study of the White House Chief of Staff function, Charles Walcott, Shirley Warshaw, and Stephen Wayne concluded:

> "In performing the gatekeeper's role, the Chief of Staff must function as an honest broker. Practically all of the chiefs and their deputies interviewed considered such a role essential. James Baker (President Reagan's Chief of Staff) was advised by a predecessor: 'Be an honest broker. Don't use the process to impose your policy views on the President.' The President needs to see all sides. He can't be blindsided."[25]

Gatekeepers do not always intentionally prevent executives from learning about problems and failures. In some cases, they simply make the wrong judgment as to the importance of a particular matter, or they underestimate the risk involved if the problem does not get surfaced at higher levels of the organization. They may think that they can handle the matter on their own, when in fact they do not have the capacity to do so. They might oversimplify the problem when they try to communicate it to others concisely. Finally, gatekeepers might place the issue on a crowded agenda, where it simply does not get the attention it deserves.

Dismissing Intuition

Some organizations exhibit an intensely analytical culture. They apply quantitative analysis and structured frameworks to solve problems and make decisions. Data rule the day; without a wealth of statistics and information, one does not persuade others to adopt his or her proposals. While fact-based problem-solving has many merits, it does entail one substantial risk. Top managers may dismiss intuitive judgments too quickly in these environments, citing the lack of extensive data and formal analysis. In many instances, managers and employees first identify potential problems because their intuition suggests that something is not quite right. Those first early warning signs do not come from a large dataset, but rather from an individual's gut. By the time the data emerge to support the conclusion that a problem exists, the organization may be facing much more serious issues.[26]

In highly analytical cultures, my research suggests that employees also may self-censor their intuitive concerns. They fear that they do not have the burden of proof necessary to surface the potential problem they have spotted. In one case, a manager told me, "I was trained to rely on data, going back to my days in business school. The data pointed in the opposite direction of my hunch that we had a problem. I relied on the data and dismissed that nagging feeling in my gut."[27]

In the Rapid Response Team study, we found that nurses often called the teams when they had a concern or felt uncomfortable, despite the lack of conclusive data suggesting that the patient was in trouble. Their hunches often proved correct. In one hospital, the initiative's leader reported to us that "In our pilot for this program, the best single predictor of a bad outcome was the nurse's concern without other vital sign abnormalities!" Before the Rapid Response Team process, most of the nurses told us that they would have felt very nervous voicing their worries simply based on their intuition. They worried that they would be criticized for coming forward without data to back up their judgments.

Lack of Training

Problems often remain hidden because individuals and teams have not been trained how to spot problems and how to communicate their concerns to others. The efficacy of the Rapid Response Team process rested, in part, on the fact that they created a list of "triggers" that nurses and other personnel could keep an eye on when caring for patients. That list made certain cues highly salient to frontline employees; it jump-started the search for problems. The hospitals also trained employees in how to communicate their concerns when they called a Rapid Response Team. Many hospitals employed a technique called SBAR to facilitate discussions about problems. The acronym stands for Situation-Background-Assessment-Recommendation. The SBAR methodology provides a way for health care personnel to discuss a patient's condition in a systematic manner, beginning with a description of the current situation and ending with a recommendation of how to proceed with testing and/or treatment. The Institute for Healthcare Improvement explains the merits of the process:

> "SBAR is an easy-to-remember, concrete mechanism useful for framing any conversation, especially critical ones, requiring a clinician's immediate attention and action. It allows for an easy and focused way to set expectations for what will be communicated and how between members of the team, which is essential for developing teamwork and fostering a culture of patient safety."[28]

The commercial aviation industry also provides extensive checklists for its pilots to review before, during, and after flights to enhance safety. It also conducts training for its flight crews regarding the cognitive and interpersonal skills required to identify and address potential safety problems in a timely and effective manner. The industry coined the term CRM—Crew Resource Management—to describe the set of principles, techniques, and skills that crew members should use to communicate and interact more effectively as a team. CRM training, which is employed extensively throughout the industry, helps crews identify potential problems and discuss them in an open and candid manner. Through CRM training, captains learn how to encourage their crew members to bring forth concerns, and crew members learn how to raise their concerns or questions in a respectful, but assertive, manner.[29]

Aviation experts credit CRM with enhancing flight safety immeasurably. In one famous incident in 1989, United Airlines Flight 232 experienced an engine failure and a breakdown of all the plane's hydraulic systems. By most accounts, no one should have survived. However, the crew managed to execute a remarkable crash landing that enabled 185 of the 296 people onboard to survive. Captain Alfred Haynes credited CRM practices with helping them save as many lives as they did.[30]

Making Tradeoffs

At times, leaders will find it difficult to distinguish the true "signals" of trouble from all the background "noise" in the environment. Chasing down all the information required to discern whether a signal represents a true threat can be very costly. False alarms will arise when people think they have spotted a problem, when in fact, no significant threat exists. Too many false alarms can begin to "dull the senses" of the organization, causing a reduction in attentiveness over time. Leaders inevitably must make tradeoffs as they hunt for problems in their organizations. They have to weigh the costs and benefits of expending time and resources to investigate a potential problem. Naturally, we do not always make the right judgments when we weigh these costs and benefits; we will choose not to further investigate some problems that turn out to be quite real and substantial.

How do the best problem-finders deal with these challenges? First, a leader does not necessarily have to consume an extraordinary amount of resources to surface and examine potential problems. Some leaders and organizations have developed speedy, low cost methods of inquiry. Toyota's "Andon cord" system represents one such highly efficient process for examining signals of potential trouble. The organization does not grind to a halt every time a front-line worker pulls the "Andon cord." Second, the best problem-finders recognize that false alarms can be remarkable learning opportunities. Moreover, making someone feel bad for triggering a false alarm can discourage him from ever coming forward again. The cost of suppressing people's voices can be far higher than the expense associated with chasing down a false alarm. For the Rapid Response Teams, the hospitals train the experts to be gentle with those who call for help when no true threat exists. They even tell them not to use the "false alarm" terminology. Instead, the experts work with people to help them refine their ability to discern true threats from less serious concerns. Finally, effective problem-finders recognize that the process of trying to uncover potential threats can have positive "spillover effects." For instance, hospitals have found that the process for investigating possible medical errors often leads to the discovery of opportunities for reducing expenses or improving patient satisfaction.

Perhaps most importantly, leaders must remember that problem-finding abilities tend to improve over time. As you practice the methods described in this book, you will become better at distinguishing the signals from the noise. You will become more adept at identifying whether a piece of information suggests a serious problem or not. The nurses, for instance, told us that experience proves to be a great teacher. Over time, they learned how to discern more accurately whether a patient could be headed for cardiac arrest. Moreover, the Rapid Response Teams became more efficient at diagnosing a patient when they arrived at the bedside. In short, costs of problem-finding do fall substantially as people practice these skills repeatedly.[31]

Becoming an Effective Problem-Finder

In the remainder of this book, we will lay out the key skills and capabilities required to ensure that problems do not remain hidden in your organization. Keep in mind that problem-finding does not precede processes of continuous improvement. Learning does not follow a linear path. Take the athlete who practices her sport on a regular basis. She does not always discover a problem first and then practice a new technique for overcoming that flaw. Sometimes, an athlete sets out on a normal practice routine, and through that process, she discovers problems that diminish her effectiveness. In sum, the processes of problem-finding and continuous improvement are inextricably linked. A person should not focus on one at the expense of the other, nor should he expect to proceed in a linear fashion from problem discovery to performance improvement. We often will discover new problems while working to solve old ones.

The following chapters explain the seven vital behaviors of effective problem finders. To discover the small problems and failures that threaten your organization, you must do the following:

- **Circumvent the gatekeepers:** Remove the filters at times, and go directly to the source to see and hear the raw data. Listen aggressively to the people actually doing the work.[32] Keep in touch with what is happening at the periphery of your business, not simply at the core.

- **Become an ethnographer:** Many anthropologists observe people in natural settings, which is known as ethnographic research. Emulate them. Do not simply ask people how things are going. Do not depend solely on data from surveys and focus groups. Do not simply listen to what people say; watch what they do—much like an anthropologist. Go out and observe how employees, customers, and suppliers actually behave. Effective problem-finders become especially adept at observing the unexpected without allowing preconceptions to cloud what they are seeing.

- **Hunt for patterns:** Reflect on and refine your individual and collective pattern-recognition capability. Focus on the efficacy of your personal and organizational processes for drawing analogies to past experiences. Search deliberately for patterns amidst disparate data points in the organization.

- **Connect the dots:** Recognize that large-scale failures often are preceded by small problems that occur in different units of the organization. Foster improved sharing of information, and build mechanisms to help people integrate critical data and knowledge. You will "connect the dots" among issues that may initially seem unrelated, but in fact, have a great deal in common.

- **Encourage useful failures:** Create a "Red Pencil Award" philosophy akin to the one at Build-a-Bear. Encourage people to take risks and to come forward when mistakes are made. Reduce the fear of failure in the organization. Help your people understand the difference between excusable and inexcusable mistakes.

- **Teach how to talk and listen:** Give groups of frontline employees training in a communication technique, such as Crew Resource Management, that helps them surface and discuss problems and concerns in an effective manner. Provide senior executives with training on how to encourage people to speak up, and then how to handle their comments and concerns appropriately.

- **Watch the game film:** Like a coach, reflect systematically on your organization's conduct and performance, as well as on the behavior and performance of competitors. Learn about and seek to avoid the typical traps that firms encounter when they engage in lessons learned and competitive-intelligence exercises. Create opportunities for individuals and teams to practice desired behaviors so as to enhance their performance, much like elite athletic performers do.

The Isolation Trap

Problem-finders do not allow themselves to become isolated from their organization and its constituents. They tear down the barriers that often arise around senior leaders. They reach out to the periphery of their business, and they engage in authentic, unscripted conversations with those people on the periphery. They set out to observe the unexpected, while discarding their preconceptions and biases.

Unfortunately, far too many senior executives of large companies become isolated in the corner office. Their professional lives involve a series of handlers—people who take their calls, screen their email, drive them places, run errands for them. They live in gated communities, travel in first class, and stay at five-star hotels. They have worked hard for these privileges; few would suggest that they don't deserve them. However, executives often find themselves living and working in a bubble. They lose touch with their frontline employees, their customers, and their suppliers.

The isolation trap does not afflict only senior leaders. Leaders at all levels sometimes find themselves isolated from those who actually know about the problems that threaten the organization. Yes, many leaders conduct town-hall meetings with employees, and they go on customer visits periodically. They tour the company factories or stores, and they visit supplier locations. However, these events are often highly orchestrated and quite predictable. People typically know that they are coming, which clearly alters the dynamic a great deal. Often, executives simply witness a nice show, put on by lower-level managers to impress them. They don't actually come to understand the needs and concerns of people who work in their factories or consume their goods. Such isolation breeds complacency and an inability to see the true problems facing the organization.

Problem-finders recognize the isolation trap, and they set out to avoid it. They put themselves out there; they open themselves to hearing about, observing, and learning about problems. Problem-finders acknowledge and discuss their own mistakes publicly. They recognize that one cannot make great decisions or solve thorny problems unless one knows about them. Novartis senior executive Larry Allgaier told me recently that he always keeps in mind an adage: "I worry the most about what my people are not telling me."[33] That statement reflects the philosophy of the successful problem-finder. They worry deeply about what they do not know. They worry deeply that they do not know what they do not know.[34]

Endnotes

[1] This disguised example is drawn from research that I conducted along with a thesis student, Jason Park, as well as Harvard Professors Amy Edmondson and David Ager. We conducted the research at four hospitals: Baptist Memorial Hospital in Memphis, St. Joseph's Hospital in Peoria, Missouri Baptist Medical Center in St. Louis, and Beth Israel Deaconess Medical Center in Boston. For more on this research, see Jason Park's award-winning 2006 Harvard College senior thesis, "Making rapid response real: Change management and organizational learning in critical patient care." During this project, Jason and I interviewed forty-nine medical professionals at the four hospitals, and we observed weekly administrative meetings at one of these hospitals for a period of several months. We would like to especially thank Nancy Sanders, R.N., from Missouri Baptist; Marla Slock, R.N., from St. Joseph's; Dr. Emmel Golden from Baptist Memorial in Memphis; and Dr. Michael Howell from Beth Israel Deaconess for their support and cooperation in our research initiative.

[2] Franklin, C., and J. Matthew. (1994). "Developing strategies to prevent in-hospital cardiac arrest: Analyzing responses of physicians and nurses in the hours before the event." *Critical Care Medicine.* 22(2): 244–247.

[3] For more on rapid response teams, see the Institute for Healthcare Improvement's How-to Guide titled "Getting Started Kit: Rapid Response Teams."

[4] Sharek, P. J., L. M. Parast, K. Leong, J. Coombs, K. Earnest, J. Sullivan, et al. (2007). "Effect of a Rapid Response Team on Hospital-wide Mortality and Code Rates Outside the ICU in a Children's Hospital." *Journal of the American Medical Association.* 298: 2267–2274.

[5] Two classic works in this regard are by sociologist Charles Perrow and psychologist James Reason. For more information, see C. Perrow. (1999). *Normal Accidents: Living with High-Risk Technologies.* Princeton, NJ: Princeton University Press, and J. Reason (1990). *Human Error.* Cambridge, England: Cambridge University Press. In his book, Reason argues that organizational accidents represent a chain of errors in most circumstances. He also puts forth his "Swiss cheese model" regarding the organizational defenses against accidents. According to this conceptual framework, an organization's layers of defense against accidents are described as slices of cheese. Reason likens the holes in the block of cheese to the weaknesses in those defenses. The holes in a block of Swiss cheese typically do not line up perfectly, such that one cannot look through a hole on one side and see through to the other side. Unfortunately, in some rare instances, the holes become completely aligned. Reason argues that a small error then can traverse the block—that is, cascade quickly through the organizational system. In most cases, though, the holes do not line up. Thus, one of the layers of defense catches a small error before it cascades throughout the system.

[6] Turner, B. A. (1976). "The organizational and interorganizational development of disasters." *Administrative Science Quarterly.* 21(3): 378–397.

[7] For a review of the literature on catastrophic failure, you might want to take a look at a recent book chapter I wrote: Roberto, M. (2008). "Why Catastrophic Organizational Failures Happen" in C. Wankel (ed.), *21st Century Management.* (pp. 471–481).Thousand Oaks, CA: Sage Publications.

[8] Edmondson, A. C. and M. D. Cannon. (2005). "Failing to Learn and Learning to Fail (Intelligently): How Great Organizations Put Failure to Work to Improve and Innovate." *Long Range Planning Journal*. 38(3): 299–320.

[9] Sim Sitkin wrote a seminal paper on the issue of how organizations can benefit from what he called "intelligent failures." These failures represent opportunities for learning that must be embraced. See Sitkin, S. B. (1996). "Learning through failure: The strategy of small losses." In M. D. Cohen and L. S. Sproull (eds.), *Organizational Learning*. (pp. 541–578).Thousand Oaks, CA: Sage.

[10] For more on Toyota's culture of continuous improvement, see Takeuchi, H., E. Osono, and Norihiko Shimizu. (2008). "The contradictions that drive Toyota's success." *Harvard Business Review*. June: 96–105; Spear, S. and Kent Bowen. (1999). "Decoding the DNA of the Toyota Production System." *Harvard Business Review*. September: 96–107.

[11] Weick, K. and Kathleen Sutcliffe. (2001). *Managing the Unexpected: Assuring High Performance in an Age of Complexity*. San Francisco: Jossey Bass. p. 56.

[12] Mishina, K. (1992). "Toyota Motor Manufacturing, U S A , Inc." *Harvard Business School Case Study No. 9-693-019*. Mishina provides an in-depth description of the Toyota Production System, including the procedure by which frontline workers can pull the Andon cord to alert supervisors of a potential problem. Mishina also describes how and why the line actually stops on some occasions when the Andon cord has been pulled.

[13] Fishman, C. (2006). "No satisfaction." *Fast Company*. 111: 82–91.

[14] Watanabe, K. (2007). "The HBR Interview: Lessons from Toyota's Long Drive." *Harvard Business Review*. July–August: 74–83.

[15] Clark, M. with A. Joyner. (2006). *The Bear Necessities of Business: Building a Company with Heart*. Hoboken, NJ: John Wiley and Sons. p. 89.

[16] Ibid, p. 92.

[17] Ibid.

[18] Amy Edmondson has written prolifically on the subject of psychological safety. For example, see Edmondson, A. (1999). "Psychological safety and learning behavior in work teams." *Administrative Science Quarterly*. 44: p. 354; Edmondson, A., R. Bohmer, and Gary Pisano. (2001). "Disrupted Routines: Team Learning and New Technology Adaptation." *Administrative Science Quarterly* 46: 685–716; Edmondson, A. (2003). "Speaking up in the Operating Room: How Team Leaders Promote Learning in Interdisciplinary Action Teams." *Journal of Management Studies* 40(6): 1419–1452; Detert, J. R. and A. C. Edmondson. (2007). "Why Employees Are Afraid to Speak Up." *Harvard Business Review*. May: 23–25.

[19] Anita Tucker and Amy Edmondson wrote an award-winning article in 2003 in which they distinguish between first-order and second-order problem-solving. In their research, they found that hospital nurses often fixed the problems they encountered on the front lines so that they could get their work done (first-order problem-solving), but they often did not dig deeper to address the underlying systemic failures (second-order problem-solving). Nurses solved the problems within their own unit,

but they did not communicate more broadly about the issues they had encountered. This isolation impeded learning and meant that problems continued to recur. See Tucker, A. and A. Edmondson. (2007). "Why Hospitals Don't Learn from Failures: Organizational and Psychological Dynamics That Inhibit System Change." *California Management Review* 45(2): 53–71.

[20] Former General Electric CEO Jack Welch describes the dangers of structural complexity in one of his books. See Welch, J. (2001). *Jack: Straight from the Gut*. New York: Warner Business Books.

[21] This section draws upon research that I conducted along with Professor Jan Rivkin of the Harvard Business School and our research associate, Erika Ferlins. See Rivkin, J. W., M. A. Roberto, and Erika Ferlins. (2006). "Managing National Intelligence (A): Before 9/11." *Harvard Business School Case Study 9-706-463*.

[22] *The 9/11 Commission Report: Final Report of the National Commission on Terrorist Attacks Upon the United States*. (2004). New York: W.W. Norton & Company. p. 353.

[23] For an excellent analysis of presidential decision-making, including the role of the chief of staff, see the following: George, A. (1980). *Presidential Decision-making in Foreign Policy: The Effective Use of Information and Advice*. Boulder, Colorado: Westview Press; Johnson, R. T. (1974). *Managing the White House*. New York: Harper Row. In addition, you might examine Stephen Ambrose's biographical work on Dwight D. Eisenhower, both as a general and as president. See Ambrose, S. E. (1990). *Eisenhower: Soldier and President*. New York: Touchstone.

[24] Walcott, C., S. Warshaw, and Stephen Wayne. (2000). "The Chief of Staff." *The White House 2001 Project: Report No. 21*. p. 1.

[25] Ibid, p. 12.

[26] In both NASA space shuttle accidents, engineers had serious concerns about the safety of the vehicle, but they could not prove their case with statistically significant data. Instead, their intuition told them that the shuttle was not safe. The NASA culture tended to downplay judgments based on instinct, instead emphasizing quantitative evidence from large datasets. For more on the *Challenger* accident, see Vaughan, D. (1996). *The Challenger Launch Decision: Risky Technology, Culture, and Deviance at NASA*. Chicago: University of Chicago Press. For more on the *Columbia* accident, see Edmondson, A., M. Roberto, R. Bohmer, E. Ferlins, and Laura Feldman. (2005). "The Recovery Window: Organizational Learning Following Ambiguous Threats." In M. Farjoun and W. Starbuck (eds.), *Organization at the Limit: Lessons from the Columbia Disaster* (220–245). London: Blackwell.

[27] Interview with a former senior executive at Bright Horizons, the employer-sponsored child care provider.

[28] http://www.ihi.org/IHI/Topics/PatientSafety/SafetyGeneral/Tools/SBARTechniqueforCommunicationASituationalBriefingModel.htm.

[29] Weiner, E. L., B. G. Kanki, and Robert L. Helmreich. (1995). *Cockpit Resource Management*. London: Academic Press.

[30] During a speech at NASA's Ames Research Center on May 24, 1991, Captain Alfred Haynes credited Crew Resource Management (CRM) techniques with helping him crash-land United Airlines Flight 232. For a copy of this speech, see the following URL: http://yarchive.net/air/airliners/dc10_sioux_city.html. For an academic interpretation of this particular incident, see McKinney, E. H., J. R. Barker, K. J. Davis, and Daryl Smith. (2005). "How Swift Starting Action Teams Get off the Ground: What United Flight 232 and Airline Flight Crews Can Tell Us About Team Communication." *Management Communication Quarterly*. 19: 198–237.

[31] For more discussion of the cost-benefit tradeoffs that problem-finders face, see Edmondson, A., M. Roberto, R. Bohmer, E. Ferlins, and Laura Feldman (2005).

[32] Retired Captain Michael Abrashoff uses the term "aggressive listening" in his book about the leadership lessons that he learned as the commander of a U.S. Navy Arleigh Burke class destroyer.

[33] Conversation with Larry Allgaier during a Novartis Customized Executive Education program at the Harvard Business School in fall 2007.

[34] Karlene Roberts is an expert on high-reliability organizations—enterprises that cope with high levels of risk on a daily basis, yet maintain very low accident rates. She argues that managers in these organizations aggressively seek to know what they don't know. See Roberts, K., R. Bea, and D. Bartles. (2001). "Must accidents happen? Lessons from high reliability organizations." *Academy of Management Executive*. 15(3): 70–79.

2

Circumvent the Gatekeepers

"Bad news isn't wine. It doesn't improve with age."
—General Colin Powell

On November 21, 1970, fifty-six American soldiers conducted an audacious raid on the secluded Son Tay prisoner of war (POW) camp, deep in the heart of North Vietnam. The planning of the operation began in May of that year, when reconnaissance imagery showed evidence of soldiers being held captive at Son Tay. One intelligence official noted, "What really grabbed our attention was another pile of rocks that had been laid out in Morse code that said there were at least six men in that prison who were going to die if they didn't get help fast."[1]

Special-operations forces trained rigorously for this mission, rehearsing a remarkable one hundred seventy times in the months leading up to the raid. The rehearsals attempted to mimic the actual conditions at Son Tay, with live-fire exercises conducted at a mock-up of the camp that was constructed at a Florida military base. U.S. Air Force personnel logged more than one thousand hours of flying time in preparation for the mission, which called for dangerous low-altitude flying by MC-130 aircraft under radio silence. Meanwhile, the U.S. Navy prepared exhaustively for an extensive diversion that they created in Haiphong Harbor on the night of the raid.

President Richard Nixon ultimately approved the mission, and the raid took place in November. The special-operations forces executed their plan with remarkable precision. The soldiers landed at the camp in the middle of the night, ready to free the seventy POWs believed to be located there. Despite the danger, no soldiers died during the raid, and only two suffered injuries. In fact, the forces killed more than one hundred enemy troops—actually Russian and Chinese advisors located at a training school adjacent to the camp. However, when the special-operations forces searched the compound, they found no POWs. The North Vietnamese had moved the prisoners prior to the raid. The incident, despite the heroic efforts of the special-operations forces, became an embarrassing example of flawed intelligence leading to faulty decision-making.

Decision-making regarding the Son Tay raid took place at the highest levels of the U.S. government. Brigadier General Donald Blackburn gave the green light for the planning and training to take place. Admiral Thomas Moorer, Chairman of the Joint Chiefs of Staff, and Secretary of Defense Melvin Laird reviewed and approved the plans. By late summer, though, imagery seemed to show decreased activity at the camp. Nevertheless, preparations for the raid continued.

In late September, Laird briefed President Nixon on the mission, who seemed to favor the idea. Laird informed Nixon about recent images that indicated decreased activity at the camp, while noting that experts continued to seek better photographs. As it turned out, many additional attempts to secure reconnaissance images during the autumn months proved unsuccessful. During this time, the planners lamented that they did not have human intelligence about the camp.

After their meeting, Nixon asked Laird to review the plans with National Security Advisor Henry Kissinger, which he did in early October. At that meeting, Kissinger asked about the risks. General Blackburn offered him a "95 to 97 percent assurance of success."[2] In his memoirs, Kissinger points out, "We knew the risk of casualties, but none of the briefings that led to the decision to proceed had ever mentioned the possibility that the camp might be empty."[3]

Finally, on November 18, Admiral Moorer and Secretary Laird met with Nixon to secure his final approval. At this meeting, Moorer and Laird did not bring up the evidence of decreased activity in the most recent photographs from late summer. Nixon gave the green light, hoping to free the prisoners and secure a boost in public support for the war and his administration. He also wanted to gain leverage at the negotiating table by showing that the U.S. could stage a successful raid deep in enemy territory. Impressed by the extensive preparations that had been done, Nixon declared, "How could anyone *not* approve this?"[4] When Moorer mentioned that the operation would be canceled at the last minute if any signs indicated that the North Vietnamese had become aware of the operation, the President replied, "Damn, Tom, let's not let *that* happen. I want this thing to go."[5]

Soon after this fateful meeting, General Blackburn received word that a North Vietnamese human-intelligence source had reported to the Central Intelligence Agency (CIA) that no prisoners remained at the Son Tay camp. They had been moved to another site. The source, a North Vietnamese bureaucrat, had worked with the U.S. for more than a year and had proven quite reliable. However, the CIA did not disclose this source to General Blackburn and his staff during the many months in which they had been planning the raid. The CIA only asked the bureaucrat about Son Tay in the days just prior to the mission, after they learned that the planners had been unable to secure high-quality imagery of the camp recently.[6]

When Blackburn received word about the source, he launched into a reassessment of the situation. Over the next twenty-four hours, he conferred with Laird, Moorer, and Lieutenant General Donald Bennett—the head of the Defense Intelligence Agency (DIA). Blackburn still wanted to go ahead, but he did not know what to make of the contradictory intelligence. He noted, "One minute they were 'sure' the prisoners were gone, the next they were 'suspicious' that POWs had been moved back into Son Tay."[7] In a key meeting on

November 20, Bennett provided roughly equal amounts of evidence both for and against the conclusion that prisoners remained at Son Tay. In the end, though, Bennett agreed that the mission should go ahead, in part based on Blackburn's assurances of success. Laird and Moorer decided to proceed as scheduled on November 21. Interestingly, Laird did not notify the White House about the human intelligence that had surfaced and the debates that had ensued among the mission's planners. An assistant to Moorer commented that Nixon "didn't want to know" about contradictory information at that point. Laird later said that he did not find the human intelligence credible, so he chose not to pass it along to the president.[8]

The story of the Son Tay raid highlights a very important challenge for leaders in all organizations. People at various levels in the organizational hierarchy filter information for various reasons. They do not pass along all the data they have received or collected. Instead, they make judgments about what information is required by their leaders to make key decisions. Leaders know that filtering takes place, and to some extent, they welcome it. After all, they do not want to become overwhelmed with data; they want their advisors to synthesize and analyze key information for them. However, leaders should worry that they may be shielded from key problems by this filtering process. Without question, the most extensive filtering tends to take place with regard to bad news, disconcerting information, and data that contradict the senior leaders' preestablished viewpoints or positions on a particular issue.

Consider the filtering that took place with regard to the Son Tay incident, and the way in which the president's behavior encouraged that filtering to take place. The CIA chose not to pass along information about its human-intelligence source until the last minute. The agency sat on that information for months. Secretary of Defense Laird chose not to inform the president of the new information from that source indicating that the prisoners had been moved to another camp. That filtering of new information took place despite the fact that, for many weeks, the planners had expressed disappointment at the lack of human intelligence on the camp. The planners finally had the information that they craved for so long, yet they deemed it unreliable and chose not to pass it along to the White House. Through it all, Nixon chose not to probe deeper when given information that some recent imagery showed reduced activity at the camp. He made it very clear that he wanted to move forward with the mission, and he stated quite firmly that he would be disappointed if they had to cancel the operation. In short, Nixon's enthusiasm for the mission seemed to discourage subordinates from coming forward with the "bad news" regarding the apparent abandonment of the camp. The president certainly never invited his advisors to come forward with any information that would disconfirm their existing view that POWs were being held at that location. He did not tell his advisors to filter out bad news, but he certainly did not create an atmosphere that welcomed discordant information. In sum, the Son Tay incident provides a vivid example of both the dangers of filtering and the leadership behaviors that can encourage the suppression of information about key problems—the bad news that no one seems to want to hear.

Why Filtering Takes Place

Why do people filter information, as Secretary Laird did in the Son Tay case? The reasons range from well-intentioned behaviors meant to help the leader to self-interested behaviors designed to advance one's own agenda.

Efficiency Concerns

First, individuals choose to summarize and package information for senior leaders for the sake of efficiency. They have a limited amount of time to spend with top executives, and they must use that time wisely. Senior leaders have asked for assistance in decision-making; they want to see key data presented, synthesized, and analyzed. In some cases, they want to see the pros and cons of various options. In others, they also want their subordinates to recommend a course of action that should be chosen. Individuals have to make tough choices about what information should be presented in the limited time frame available. "Face time" with senior leaders becomes a precious commodity, and no one wants to squander it by inundating them with information that is not organized and analyzed properly. Neither leaders nor subordinates want to spend time on information that is irrelevant or unreliable. Busy schedules and crowded meeting agendas certainly exacerbate the amount of filtering that takes place. Given the fast pace within most organizations, individuals know that they must get to the point in meetings.[9]

Individuals also do not know want to waste senior leaders' time with problems that they believe can and should be solved without executive assistance. Many people fear that they will appear weak or, worse yet, incompetent if they bring a problem to a higher level in the organization. They dread being asked why they could not resolve the issue on their own, or why they are "wasting leadership's time" on issues that appear to be insignificant.

Pressures for Conformity

Individuals also filter information when a group of senior leaders has arrived at an apparent consensus fairly quickly. In those cases, individuals may feel pressure to conform to the majority viewpoint.[10] At that point, one may not want to introduce information into the discussion that unsettles or challenges the dominant perspective. Subordinates often do not want to be perceived as rabble-rousers, intent on upsetting the apple cart at the final hour.

Leaders create pressures for conformity whenever they foster the impression that they have already made up their mind. If they stop demonstrating a genuine curiosity and a desire to learn more about a situation, they encourage filtering of discordant information. In the Son Tay case, Nixon signaled very strongly that he would like to proceed with the mission. He did not seem concerned when told that the later images showed decreased activity at the camp. People involved in the White House meetings indicated that he did not seem curious to know why that was the case. Moreover, when Admiral Moorer said that he would recommend canceling the mission if new information arose suggesting that the secrecy of the operation had been compromised, Nixon replied, "Damn, Tom, let's not let *that* happen. I want this thing to *go*."[11] In short, he signaled very strongly that he did not want additional information that might cause reconsideration of the decision to proceed.

When a leader seems to have his or her mind made up, subordinates make a rational calculation with an eye toward future decisions. They want to have an opportunity to influence future choices; they do not want to lose a seat at the table. To preserve access, power, and influence, individuals determine when senior leaders no longer want to hear about additional information pertaining to the decision at hand. At that point, subordinates trade off a possible reduction in quality of the current choice for the maintenance of their role in future decision-making processes.

Confirmation Bias

Filtering sometimes takes place in a rather unconscious manner. Psychologists have shown that human beings tend to process information in a biased manner. We tend to seek out information that confirms our existing views and hypotheses, and we tend to avoid or even discount data that might disconfirm our current positions on particular issues. Psychologists describe this tendency as the confirmation bias.[12]

We do not always sense that we have assimilated information in a biased manner. Moreover, we enact this bias in a variety of fashions— some more direct than others. Clearly, we may act in a biased manner in our own personal efforts to gather and analyze data. We also might invite certain people to meetings, and not invite others, based on an inclination as to what those people believe. However, the confirmation bias may play out in more subtle ways too. For instance, we may call on people in a certain order in a meeting, such that momentum clearly builds for a particular option through the repeated presentation of data that bolster the preferred alternative. We may even arrange seating in a conference room such that people who are believed to hold disconfirming information do not have the opportunity to sit next to the key decision-maker(s). The lack of physical proximity may send a strong signal about power relationships and thus discourage the bringing forth of information that does not confirm the existing view of the world within that room.

Kissinger apparently recognized that confirmation bias affected the decision-making process in the Son Tay incident. In his memoirs, he wrote, "A President, and even more his National Security Adviser, must take nothing on faith; they must question every assumption and probe every fact. Not everything that is plausible is true, for those who put forward plans for action have a *psychological disposition* to marshal the facts that support their position." [emphasis added][13]

Advocacy

Filtering naturally may occur for purely self-interested reasons in some cases. Advocates for a particular position may provide information in a manner designed to bolster their recommendation and persuade others to support them.[14] At the same time, they may withhold information that highlights the risks and costs of their proposed course of action. To his credit, Lieutenant General Bennett did not do this when offering his intelligence assessment to Blackburn, Moorer, and Laird in that final meeting before the Son Tay mission began. Instead, he offered a balanced view, with apparently equal amounts of data both in support of and against going ahead. However, Blackburn clearly seemed to tilt his presentations throughout the process in favor of moving forward with the mission. Laird, too, became a strong advocate for the operation, rather than an unbiased evaluator of the mission's benefits and risks. While he had informed Nixon of the evidence of reduced activity at the camp in prior meetings, he did not bring that data forward again when asking the president for final approval to proceed with the operation on November 18. Of course, Laird also did not go back to the president with the human intelligence.

Circumventing the Filters

If leaders hope to uncover key problems in their organizations before they mushroom into large-scale failures, they must understand why subordinates may choose to filter out bad news. They must be wary of how their own behavior may cause their advisors to hold back dissonant information. Leaders clearly must create a climate in which people feel comfortable coming forward with new data, even data that might go against the dominant view in the organization. To become effective and proactive problem-finders, though, leaders must go one step further. From time to time, leaders must circumvent the filters by reaching out beyond their direct reports to look at raw data, speaking directly with key constituents, and learning from those with completely different perspectives than their closest advisors. In short, leaders need to occasionally "open the funnel" that typically synthesizes, packages, and constricts the information flow up the hierarchy. They have to reach down and out, beyond the executive suite and even beyond the walls of the organization, to access new data directly. They have to find information that has not been massaged and packaged into a neat, slick Microsoft PowerPoint presentation. To do so, leaders must become adept at five techniques shown in Table 2.1.

These activities may take some time amidst an already very busy schedule for senior executives, but the investment will pay off handsomely if it enables leaders to spot threats, as well as opportunities, at a very early stage.

TABLE 2.1   Five Strategies for Circumventing the Filters

Strategy	Description
Listen with your own ears	Create regular opportunities for direct, candid conversations between key constituents and senior leaders. Hold executives accountable for responding to the concerns they hear.
Seek different voices	Rotate responsibilities for key reports and presentations. Ask to meet with different people from lower levels of the organization. Seek out the people who actually do the work or use the product.
Connect with young people	Seek out the youngest and the brightest inside and outside your organization. Use them to learn about new trends and gain access to a different worldview.
Go to the periphery	Communicate with employees in distant geographic regions, units exploring new technology, or small new ventures trying to get off the ground outside the firm's core market. Focus on the disconnects between what people are saying at the core versus the periphery of the business.
Talk to the nons	Make it a habit to speak with noncustomers, nonemployees, and nonsuppliers—those who choose not to interact with the organization for some reason.

Listen with Your Own Ears

Anne Mulcahy took over as CEO at Xerox on August 1, 2001. She became CEO at a time when the organization was in deep trouble. Losses had mounted, the sales force seemed dispirited, and the debt burden was overwhelming. A Securities and Exchange Commission (SEC) investigation ultimately led to a restatement of earnings going back to 1997. The specter of bankruptcy loomed. Over the past seven years, Mulcahy has engineered a remarkable transformation. She has reconfigured and enhanced the company's product line, enhanced customer service, and returned the company to a sound financial position.[15]

Mulcahy has taken some interesting steps to ensure that she and her fellow senior executives receive unfiltered information about customer satisfaction and dissatisfaction. She has chosen to listen directly to them, without a go-between who might alter or muddy the message. Specifically, Mulcahy employs two techniques to circumvent the usual filtering process that shapes the customer-service data that reach senior leaders. Her techniques involve more than simply going out on customer visits, although she does that as well. First, Mulcahy has assigned each of the company's top five hundred customers to a member of the top management team. Interestingly, she has not assigned accounts only to executives in charge of functions such as sales, marketing, and operations. She explains:

> "All our executives are involved—including our Chief Accountant, our General Counsel and our head of Human Resources. Each executive is responsible for communicating with at least one of our customers, understanding their concerns and requirements and making sure the appropriate Xerox resources are marshaled to fix problems, address issues and capture opportunities."[16]

Secondly, Mulcahy has created a program whereby each member of the top management team serves as a "Customer Officer of the Day" at corporate headquarters on a monthly basis. She wants to hear the unvarnished comments from customers who may be having problems with the firm's products. Moreover, Mulcahy wants each member of the top team, including herself, to be personally accountable for addressing customer concerns. She describes the program:

> "There are about 20 of us and we rotate responsibility to be 'Customer Officer of the Day.' It works out to about a day a month. When you're in the box, you assume personal responsibility for dealing with any and all customer complaints, that come in to headquarters that day. They are usually from customers who have had a bad experience. They're angry. They're frustrated. And they're calling headquarters as their course of last resort. The Xerox 'Officer of the Day' has three responsibilities—listen to the customer, resolve their problem and assume responsibility for fixing the underlying cause. Believe me, it keeps us in touch with the real world. It grounds us. It permeates all our decision making."[17]

Mulcahy's initiatives create direct communication between front-line users of her products and senior executives. She does not simply rely on summaries of statistics about customer service. The conversations with customers become valuable raw data that may provide insights not available in reports compiled from reams of customer survey statistics. Mulcahy has learned that customer questionnaires can be deceiving. People may report that they are "satisfied" with a company on a survey, yet still remain quite likely to switch to another firm's products. Mulcahy describes this phenomenon:

> "There has been a norm around for many years that some-where around 75 per cent of customers who defect say they were 'satisfied.' Our own research bears this out. When our customers tell us they are 'very satisfied,' they are six times more likely to continue doing business with us than those who are merely satisfied... If you're just providing your customers with service that's good, they're probably just satisfied. This should set off alarm bells. Take the automotive industry. Satisfaction scores average around 90 per cent. Guess how many people repurchase from the same manufacturer? Only 40 per cent."[18]

CVS is another company that has found ways for senior executives to access unfiltered information about customer service. In the past, the company relied on mystery shoppers to evaluate service in each of its store locations. Today, CVS has a program called Triple S, which stands for stock, shop, and service. Are the products that customers want in stock? Are the stores neat, clean, and uncluttered? Are the store associates courteous, helpful, and professional, and are wait times minimized? The company measures the three Ss using a customer questionnaire. People who shop at CVS occasionally receive a receipt for their purchases that contains an invitation to call a toll-free number and respond to a set of survey questions. Customers who respond become eligible for a cash sweepstakes that takes place each month. Today, CVS receives more than one million responses per year from its customers. The company finds that a store's sales performance is correlated with its Triple S score.

Interestingly, though, CVS does more than simply compile Triple S scores for each of its stores. Executives do not only look at reports filled with analysis of the data. Helena Foulkes, Senior Vice President of Marketing, explains that the calls are recorded, and that executives can listen to actual comments for a particular store that appears to be struggling. Moreover, CVS has enacted a "Customer Comment of the Day" program for its senior leadership team. Each day, the top ten executives at CVS receive an electronic audio file of one phone call received the prior day from a customer. That comment can be either positive or negative. A senior manager typically selects this call to distribute to the top team because it highlights something new or intriguing that they may not have considered or heard previously. Foulkes finds some of these comments to be incredibly thought provoking. Finally, similar to Xerox, each senior team member takes calls from customers for one hour roughly twice per year. Foulkes points out that these recorded and live phone calls are "deeply personal" experiences. They shed insights in a way that quantitative data sometimes do not. She also points out that they provide a perspective that an executive cannot achieve simply by shopping in or walking the firm's stores. Foulkes explains that, "The way that you shop as a retailer is quite different than the way that your customers shop." As a result, executives and customers experience the stores in distinct ways. It proves difficult to see the stores through a customer's eyes. Foulkes stresses that listening to the Customer Comment of the Day and taking phone calls personally enables executives to hear about problems firsthand, to spot patterns and trends quickly, and to avoid becoming isolated in the executive suite.[19]

Seek Different Voices

In 2005, David Tacelli became the CEO of LTX Corporation, a producer of semiconductor test equipment located in Norwood, Massachusetts. Tacelli has implemented a rigorous customer review system to review the company's major accounts on a regular basis. He aims to "surface customer service problems early" through this routine evaluation process. He has learned, though, that the system can become stale if the same senior manager reports on a particular customer at each review meeting. As he says, "They tend to filter. They think that they can fix the problem. Therefore, they do not tell anyone until far too late."[20] Therefore, Tacelli makes sure that everyone involved with a particular client presents over time at these review meetings. He explains:

> "I rotate presenters very purposefully. If a problem surfaces at a particular meeting, I will go back to the person that presented at the previous meeting. I ask them if they were aware of the issue at the time of their presentation. If so, then I probe as to why they did not surface the issue sooner. The key is for them to learn from the experience and not make this an exercise to assign blame. I'm trying to teach them to communicate openly about issues so we can solve them more effectively. Of course, I do look for patterns of mistakes from people who present. If someone repeatedly holds back information, then I need to solve a different problem with that individual, because in the end, they need to know that they will be held accountable."[21]

Tacelli asks his managers to limit the number of slides they present at these meetings. He says, "I want them to talk with me and one another, not to read off of slides." He explains that his role is to "play *Jeopardy* with them...to use the Socratic method to find out what the key issues are, to see what we know about the causes of particular customer complaints."[22]

Larry Hayward seeks different voices over time as well. Hayward, a business unit general manager at Ametek Corporation, makes customer visits on a regular basis, as many executives do. However, Hayward makes it a point to speak not only with the people at the client location with whom he normally communicates by phone or email. He seeks out others in the purchasing department with whom he typically does not interact. Much more importantly, he does not restrict himself to the procurement unit. Hayward reserves time to meet with engineers, who use his firm's products on a daily basis, as well as others in various areas of the client organization. He wants to collect a variety of perspectives on his organization's products and customer service. Hayward also does not restrict himself to senior managers. He wants to speak with frontline engineers who have firsthand knowledge about the use of his firm's products.[23]

Peni Garber serves as a partner at ABRY Partners, a Boston private-equity firm specializing in the media and communication industries. She applies this same logic to her investments in various companies. When Garber visits companies that are in her investment portfolio, she makes it a point to not restrict her conversations to the CEO and other board members. Garber seeks out information from a variety of managers within the portfolio company. She does so for three reasons. First, she wants to assess the talent within the firm. Second, these conversations help her test for organizational alignment. Does everyone understand the strategy? Has senior leadership achieved strong buy-in at all levels? Do people share a common set of values? Finally and perhaps more importantly, she hopes to discover if issues are festering beneath the surface, about which the CEO and board may be unaware, or have chosen not to disclose fully to the investors. In most cases, like Tacelli at LTX, she finds that executives do not mean any harm when they hold back bad news. They believe that they can solve the problem on their own, if only they had a bit more time. They do not want to waste the investors' time with an issue that they believe can be solved quite readily.[24]

Connect with Young People

Young people often have a keen early understanding of important societal trends. They tend to have great familiarity with the latest ideas and products in fields such as technology, fashion, healthy living, and the environment. For that reason, Gary Hamel argues that CEOs should go out of their way to stay connected with the youngest and brightest in their organization. He recommends that CEOs form a "shadow cabinet" of highly capable employees in their twenties and thirties. The CEO should then meet with this cabinet periodically to see how their perspective on key strategic issues differs from what he or she is hearing from the members of the senior management team. Hamel believes that interacting with young people will help CEOs see opportunities and threats that senior leaders may not perceive. Moreover, Hamel recognizes that the perspectives of these young people often are filtered out if left to the normal machinations of the organizational hierarchy.[25]

General Electric went one step further during the e-commerce revolution of the mid- to late 1990s. One business unit president in London recognized that he did not understand the Internet as well as he should have. He wanted to get up to speed on the business. Therefore, he found the brightest young person under the age of thirty in the organization, and he asked that employee to serve as his mentor on e-commerce issues. The talented young person spent the next several months schooling the head of the business. When Jack Welch heard about this technique, he asked all the general managers at General Electric to find young mentors who could teach them the ins and outs of the web. As Welch said, "we turned the organization upside down. We had the youngest and brightest teaching the oldest."[26]

Today we find many business leaders tapping into the perspectives and ideas of young people through technology. A variety of innovations have provided a fast and economical way for senior executives to connect with young people on the front lines of their organizations. Many CEOs have blogs, and some have begun to spend time trying to understand, in a systematic manner, what their employees are writing on their own blogs. At Hewlett-Packard, researchers have created new technology that analyzes what is being written on the blogs of more than ten thousand employees. The technology, termed WaterCooler, aims to identify key issues being discussed in a particular time period, as well as patterns of comments over time. The name for the software came from the notion that it provides an ability to listen in, with permission, on the many virtual water cooler conversations that employees are having in cyberspace.[27]

Some CEOs have ventured onto Facebook and MySpace to interact with their younger employees. Paul Levy, CEO of the Beth Israel Deaconess Medical Center, has created a Facebook page. He has over four hundred friends in a social group that he has created, many of whom are his employees. He comments, "It's fun, a nice way to communicate with a group of people who might not otherwise interact with me."[28] Similarly, Tom Glocer, CEO of Thomson Reuters, spends time on Facebook. Some in the British press have criticized him for spending his time in such a manner. He offers a rebuttal—on his blog, of course:

> "Now it could be argued, I suppose, that imagination and experimentation should be left to more junior or younger staff, and the chief executive should only perform 'serious' duties like strategy formulation and ordering people around. I think this is a lousy and disconnected way to lead. I believe that unless one interacts with and plays with the leading technology of the age, it is impossible to dream the big dreams, and difficult to create an environment in which creative individuals will feel at home...I believe it is a very worthy investment of my 'free' time to explore the latest interactions of media and technology."[29]

Go to the Periphery

Andy Grove, longtime chairman and CEO of Intel, argues that senior executives must reach out to the periphery of the organization if they want to see threats and opportunities at a nascent stage. By the periphery, he means distant geographic regions, units exploring new technology, or small new ventures trying to get off the ground outside the firm's core market. Grove explains:

"Think of it this way: when spring comes, snow melts first at the periphery, because that's where it's most exposed... In the ordinary course of business, I talk with the general manager, with the sales manager, with the manufacturing manager. I learn from them what goes on in the business. But they will give me a perspective from a position that is not terribly far from my own. When I absorb news and information coming from people who are geographically distant or who are several levels below me in the organization, I will triangulate on business issues with their view, which comes from a completely different perspective. This will bring insights that I would not likely get from my ordinary contacts."[30]

In his latest research, Joseph Bower argues that chief executives may even find highly capable successors at the periphery of their organizations.[31] Bower reconsiders the notion of hiring an insider versus an outsider as the new chief executive. An insider offers the benefit of a wealth of experience in the business and a deep understanding of the firm's culture and values. However, insiders may be too tightly wedded to a particular mental model of how to do business. That cognitive inflexibility might not serve the firm well if it experiences a major shift in the external environment. Outsiders clearly bring a fresh perspective, but they may not always have the adequate experience or fit the firm's culture.[32] Bower notes that many successful succession processes involve the hiring of an executive who has spent extensive time at the periphery of the organization, working in foreign markets, new ventures, and the like. In so doing, they have developed fresh perspectives and perhaps even come to question some of the central tenets held by those who work at the core of the business. Bower describes these individuals as inside-outside leaders, and he argues that they bring a more objective perspective on the changes needed in the mainstream business when they become chief executive. In so doing, they combine the benefits of being an insider with the divergent perspective of an outsider.

Talk to the Nons

Many executives spend time talking with their current customers, employees, and suppliers. How many speak on occasion with their non-customers, nonemployees, and nonsuppliers—those who are currently not engaged with their organization in some fashion? Connecting with these groups can provide incredible insight. Clayton Christensen argues, for instance, that spotting disruptive innovation opportunities tends to happen when one speaks with noncustomers as opposed to current users. The latter group often focuses on incremental improvement ideas for your current product line, rather than a truly break-through change.[33] Likewise, speaking with applicants who have turned down a job offer from your company may tell you a great deal about how and why you can attract and retain talent more effectively. You may even go so far as to talk with university students who have attended an information session held by your firm, but then chose not to submit a job application. What did they hear or learn that caused them to look elsewhere for employment?

Universities spend a great deal of time speaking with those who choose not to become their students, and they learn an immense amount from them. Without question, every college obsesses about its admissions yield—the percentage of accepted students who choose to matriculate at the school. Yield represents a critical measure of a school's attractiveness. Moreover, poor yield prediction can have per-nicious consequences for a university. A lower-than-expected yield leads to empty dorms and the associated drop in revenue, while a higher-than-expected yield causes overcrowding and perhaps subse-quent student dissatisfaction. Universities spend time trying to speak with accepted students who chose to enroll elsewhere. They ask many questions. What other schools did they select most often? Why did they choose those schools? What types of students are most likely to not enroll? The systematic analysis of these answers often proves illuminating, and it leads to enhancements both in the admissions process and the university as a whole in the years to come. Like these schools, business leaders can benefit by speaking with those who have rejected their organization. But don't leave this task to only your customer-service personnel or human-resources managers. Senior leaders need to occasionally hear from these voices directly. They need to hear the unvarnished truth from those who have chosen not to engage with the organization for one reason or another.[34]

A Most Prescient Leader

Is finding a way to circumvent the filters truly valuable? Can it really help leaders see the future, to spot problems before they mushroom into catastrophes? To close this chapter, consider for a moment the remarkable career of Winston Churchill. Many people marvel at how prescient he was at key moments in his lifetime. He seemed to see looming threats long before others did. Time after time, he tried to sound the alarm about threats to his beloved Britain, and he recommended preparatory measures. Churchill foretold the threat from rising German militarism in the years prior to World War I. Similarly, he tried to sound alarms about the threat from Hitler during the 1930s, but sadly, his warnings fell on deaf ears for far too long. Finally, he predicted the threat from Soviet expansionism, culminating in his famous Iron Curtain speech in March 1946.

How did Churchill cultivate this ability to spot the threats and problems that loomed ahead? One reason may be that he immersed himself in each job he held in the British government. He did not spend his time huddled in London with only his closest advisors. Churchill always wanted to be in the thick of the action. He traveled relentlessly to speak with people far and wide, from inside and outside government. He demonstrated a remarkable inquisitiveness and curiosity, and he loved speaking with the people on the front lines. Some characterized him as reckless at times; he even wanted to observe the D-day landings firsthand from a naval vessel in June 1944.

General Eisenhower and King George VI intervened to keep him from doing so for safety reasons. Nevertheless, Churchill's desire to see and hear things firsthand served as an asset far more than a liability.

Consider what happened when Churchill became First Lord of the Admiralty in 1911. He set out to understand the scope of German military superiority and to revolutionize the British Navy in preparation for war. During this time, he launched a massive construction campaign and switched the British fleet from coal to oil—momentous decisions that met with a healthy dose of skepticism at the time. He also equipped his ships with 15-inch guns, an innovation that proved critical during the combat that soon unfolded.

Churchill came to these decisions after engrossing himself in all facets of the British Navy. He engaged in a whirlwind of activity:

> "With the Admiralty's yacht, the Enchantress, as his home and office, he mastered every detail of navy tactics and capabilities. He appeared to be everywhere at once, inquiring, badgering, learning. He was interested in everything from gunnery to the morale of his soldiers. He was fascinated with airplanes and immediately understood their utility for warfare. He spent hundreds of hours learning how to fly. He crawled into the cramped quarters of gun turrets and learned how they worked. It became his practice to solicit information and opinions from junior officers and ordinary seamen, often ignoring or arguing with their superiors. The respect he showed them, and the increases in pay he won for them, made him a favorite in the ranks."[35]

Churchill could get into trouble at times. His senior naval officers often did not like the fact that he asked sailors to tell him what their superiors were doing wrong. They believed that he was inviting insubordination. Without question, Churchill could have taken more care in how he gathered unfiltered information from the ranks. Nevertheless, his behavior proves instructive for us today. Churchill understood that the constriction of information that takes place in any hierarchy can be stifling—even dangerous. He understood that a leader's greatest assets sometimes are his own eyes and ears. One's closest advisors may certainly provide sound counsel in trying times, but they also may insulate a leader from the hard truths, unwelcome news, and lurking dangers that could imperil a business. Sometimes, leaders need to walk outside without an umbrella and feel the raindrops on their skin.

Endnotes

[1] Amidon, M. (2005). "Groupthink, Politics, and the Decision to Attempt the Son Tay Rescue." *Parameters: U.S. Army War College Quarterly*. 35(3): 119–131. For more information on the Son Tay raid, see Schemmer, B. F. (2002). *The Raid: The Son Tay Prison Rescue Mission*. New York: Ballantine Books.

[2] Amidon, M. (2005).

[3] Kissinger, H. (1979). *White House Years*. Boston: Little Brown. p. 982.

[4] Amidon, M. (2005).

[5] Amidon, M. (2005).

[6] The failure to share information freely among agencies of the federal government represents a recurring issue in American history. As noted in Chapter 1, a lack of information-sharing contributed to the government's failure to prevent the terrorist attacks of September 11, 2001. We will explore the circumstances surrounding those attacks in much more depth in Chapter 5. Of course, one should note that many organizations, in both the public and private sector, have "silos" that do not collaborate effectively with one another. The problem may be particularly acute in our intelligence community, but it certainly is not exclusive to those organizations.

[7] Amidon, M. (2005).

[8] For more on President Richard Nixon's leadership style, see the following books: Ambrose, S. E. (1987). *Nixon*. New York: Simon and Schuster; Reeves, R. (2002). *President Nixon: Alone in the White House*. New York: Simon and Schuster.

[9] Heike Bruch and Sumantral Ghoshal wrote an interesting article on the crowded schedules of many managers based on a decade of research on how managers spend their time. They discovered that nine out of ten managers use their time very ineffectively. Only 10% of managers "spend their time in a committed, purposeful, and reflective manner." They offer strategies for helping managers gain control of their schedules so as to be more efficient and effective. See Bruch, H. and S. Ghoshal. (2002). "Beware the Busy Manager." *Harvard Business Review*. February: 62–68.

[10] An expansive literature describes social pressures for conformity that arise in groups and organizations. Psychologist Solomon Asch conducted one of the earliest studies that had a major influence on future scholars. See Asch, S. E. (1951). "Effects of group pressure upon the modification and distortion of judgment." In

H. Guetzkow (ed.). *Groups, Leadership and Men.* (pp. 177–190). Pittsburgh: Carnegie Press. Social psychologist Irving Janis produced a classic study on the pressures for conformity within groups, based on his analysis of presidential decision-making. See Janis, I. (1982). *Victims of Groupthink.* 2nd edition. Boston: Houghton Mifflin. For some more recent work on conformity pressures, see Epley, N. and T. Gilovich. (1999). "Just going along: Nonconscious priming and conformity to social pressure." *Journal of Experimental Social Psychology.* 35: 578–589.

[11] Amidon, M. (2005).

[12] Peter Wason was one of the pioneers in research on the confirmation bias. For instance, see Wason, P. (1960). "On the failure to eliminate hypotheses in a conceptual task." *Quarterly Journal of Experimental Psychology.* 12: 129–140. A Stanford study in the late 1970s argued that confirmation bias may explain why people might examine the very same set of mixed evidence on a matter, yet come away with attitudes that are more polarized than at the outset. The authors examined people's attitudes regarding the death penalty. They found that individuals became even more entrenched in their opinions after examining a mixed set of evidence. They argued that people tended to focus on the information that confirmed their existing attitudes and beliefs, and they dismissed the data that challenged their preexisting beliefs. Thus, attitudes became more polarized. For more on this study, see Lord, C., L. Ross, and M. Lepper. (1979). "Biased assimilation and attitude polarization: The effects of prior theories on subsequently considered evidence." *Journal of Personality and Social Psychology.* 37(11): 2098–2109. For a thorough review of research on the confirmation bias, see Nickerson, R. (1998). "Confirmation bias: An ubiquitous phenomenon in many guises." *Review of General Psychology.* 2(2): 175–220.

[13] Kissinger, H. (2003). *Ending the Vietnam War.* New York: Simon and Schuster. p. 185.

[14] David Garvin and I have written an article about dysfunctional advocacy in group decision-making. See Garvin, D. and M. Roberto. (2001). "What you don't know about making decisions." *Harvard Business Review.* September: 108–119.

[15] For more on Mulcahy's turnaround at Xerox, see Kharif, O. "Anne Mulcahy Has Xerox by the Horns." *Business Week Online.* May 29, 2003. To read the entire article, see the following URL: http://www.businessweek.com/technology/content/may2003/tc20030529_1642_tc111.htm.

[16] Anne Mulcahy. "The Customer Connection: Strategies for Winning and Keeping Customers." Speech to the Empire Club of Canada. June 10, 2004. For a complete text of the speech, see the following URL: http://www.empireclubfoundation.com/details.asp?SpeechID=3000&FT=yes.

[17] Ibid.

[18] Ibid.

[19] Interview with Helena Foulkes, Senior Vice President of Marketing and Operations Services, CVS Caremark Corporation.

[20] Interview with David Tacelli, President and Chief Executive Officer, LTX Corporation.

[21] Ibid.

[22] Ibid.

[23] Interview with Larry Hayward, Vice President and General Manager, AMETEK Chemical Products.

[24] Interview with Peni Garber, Partner, ABRY Partners, LLC.

[25] Hamel, G. (2003). "The quest for resilience." *Harvard Business Review*. September: 52–58.

[26] Bartlett, C. (2000). "GE Compilation: Jack Welch—1981–99." Harvard Business School Video No. 300-512.

[27] McGregor, J. (2008). "Mining the office chatter." *Business Week*. May 19, 2008.

[28] Diaz, J. "Facebook's squirmy chapter." *Boston Globe*. April 16, 2008. For more information on Paul Levy's leadership at the Beth Israel Deaconess Medical Center, see the multimedia case study I coauthored with Professor David Garvin. The case provides a detailed account of Levy's turnaround of the medical center, which was on the verge of collapse when he took over in January 2002. The case proves unique because we collected data on the turnaround in real time by conducting video interviews with Mr. Levy every three weeks or so during the first six months of the turnaround. Those interviews began after only one week of his tenure at the hospital. We also collected hundreds of email communications and tracked press coverage of the turnaround; the case includes many of these documents as well. See Garvin, D. and M. Roberto. (2003). "Paul Levy: Taking Charge of the Beth Israel Deaconess Medical Center (A)." Harvard Business School Case No. 9-303-008. In addition, we have written an article about the leadership lessons from this turnaround. Garvin, D. and M. Roberto (2005). "Change through persuasion." *Harvard Business Review*. February: 104–112.

[29] Reed, S. "Media giant or media muddle." *Business Week*. May 1, 2008. For direct access to Glocer's blog, go to the following URL: http://tomglocer.com/.

[30] Grove, A. (1999). *Only the Paranoid Survive*. New York: Currency/Doubleday. p. 110.

[31] Bower, J. (2007). *The CEO Within: Why Inside Outsiders Are the Key to Succession Planning*. Boston: Harvard Business School Press.

[32] An extensive literature has debated the merits of hiring insiders versus outsiders as CEOs, and much empirical work has been done. For example, see the following academic studies: Behn, B., D. Dawley, R. Riley, and Y. Yang. (2006). "Deaths of CEOs: Are Delays in Naming Successors and Insider/Outsider Succession Associated with Subsequent Firm Performance?" *Journal of Managerial Issues*. 18(1): 32–47; Chen, W. and A. Cannella. (2002). "Power dynamics within top management teams and their impact on CEO dismissal following insider succession." *Academy of Management Journal*. 45: 1195–2007; Chung, K., R. Rogers, M. Lubatkin, and J. Owens. (1987). "Do Insiders Make Better CEOs Than Outsiders?" *Academy of Management Executive*. 1(4): 325–331.

[33] Christensen, C. (2000). *The Innovator's Dilemma*. New York: Harper Collins.

[34] This section on university admissions draws upon knowledge gathered from conversations over the years with Michelle Beauregard, Director of Admission at Bryant University, and Kim Clark, former Dean of the Harvard Business School.

[35] McCain, J. "Extraordinary foresight made Winston Churchill great." *The Daily Telegraph*. March 20, 2008. This article in the London newspaper was an excerpt from a book by John McCain and Mark Salter. See McCain, J. and M. Salter. (2007). *Hard Call: The Art of Great Decisions*. New York: Twelve Publishing. For more details on Churchill's leadership style, you may refer to one of the many excellent biographies that have been written. I particularly enjoyed the biography authored by British politician and writer Roy Jenkins several years ago. See Jenkins, R. (2001). *Churchill. A Biography*. New York: Farrar, Straus and Giroux.

3

Become an Ethnographer

"You can observe a lot just by watching."
—Yogi Berra

In the past, companies relied heavily on focus groups to conduct marketing research. They brought consumers to their offices, and they asked them for extensive feedback on new products and services before going to market. Today, many firms have shifted their approach, relying less on focus groups and much more on direct observation of how consumers behave in their natural environments—in their homes, workplaces, automobiles, and the like. For example, consider Kimberly Clark, producer of the Huggies brand of diapers and related baby-care products. The firm's researchers have learned a great deal by watching many parents changing their babies. During one study, they realized that most moms and dads struggled to hold their babies still while reaching for the diaper, wipes, articles of clothing, and the like. The problem became particularly acute for parents who were "on the go," changing their infants at a location outside the home. Therefore, the firm redesigned its travel pack for Huggies Baby Wipes. The new packaging enables parents to remove a wipe with only one hand, thus enabling the moms and dads to always keep their other hand on the child. Similarly, the company's researchers watched as parents had difficulty opening Huggies Baby Wash while bathing their children. Again, the moms and dads had only one hand free, as the other hand tried to prevent the infant from falling over in the bathtub.

Thus, the firm redesigned the bottle so that a parent could open it and dispense the liquid with only one hand.[1]

Other firms derive new product ideas from similar observational studies of consumer behavior. Microsoft visits consumers' homes and watches them work and play on their personal computers. The firm provides families with free hardware and software. In return, it gains permission to observe how they use these products over a lengthy period of time (observations every few months for two years in some instances). General Mills watches how people consume and shop for their products. The firm even operates its own grocery store, called the Corner Market. The general public cannot shop there; instead, General Mills invites and reimburses consumers to shop there while the firm's researchers observe them. Arm & Hammer, the producer of baking soda and related odor-control products, visits consumers' homes and observes everything from their refrigerators to their litter boxes. In one study, they noticed many cat owners failing to spot large clumps of wet litter. Therefore, they developed a new product that turns blue when damp so that homeowners can know when it's time to clean the litter box.[2]

Proctor & Gamble has developed one of the most extensive observational research programs in the world. The firm's CEO, A. G. Lafley, learned the value of watching how consumers behave, rather than simply asking them what they want, when he accepted an assignment in Japan in the early 1990s. At the time, he did not have access to extensive market research data in Japan. He had to find another way to learn what product innovations would meet consumers' needs. He remembers concluding, "Executives in the U.S. were buried under consumer research data. I don't think the answers are just in the numbers. You have to get out and look."[3]

Today, Proctor & Gamble's employees immerse themselves in their customers' lives through two innovative programs. In the firm's Livin' It initiative, employees visit people in their homes, and they join them on trips to the supermarket. In the Workin' It program, employees spend time behind the checkout counters at various retail stores. As Lafley puts it, "Richer, more actionable insights are identified from what is learned in the context of the real world."[4] The firm has increased its expenditures on such immersive research techniques by more than 500% over the past decade.[5]

Marketing experts describe this type of observational work as ethnographic research. The term comes from the fields of anthropology and sociology. Ethnographers, such as noted cultural anthropologist Margaret Mead, study groups, organizations, and cultures through close observation of people in their natural environment. In her famous work *Coming of Age in Samoa*, Mead wrote about the lives of adolescent girls and their transition to adulthood. She immersed herself in the Samoan society for five months in the 1920s, and from her systematic observations, she wrote a groundbreaking book about how culture impacts the socioemotional development of young people.[6] Today, ethnographers study not only other cultures, but also a range of other phenomena, from workers in business organizations to members of street gangs.[7]

Why have marketers adopted the methodology of Mead and her fellow ethnographers? Pure and simple, they understand that people often say one thing and do another. Asking individuals questions in focus groups may yield answers that are inconsistent with how those consumers actually behave in their homes or at retail stores. Marketing scholar Gerald Zaltman, a critic of focus-group techniques, notes that "The correlation between stated intent and actual behavior is usually low and negative."[8] He points out that 80% of new product launches fail, despite being evaluated through focus-group techniques. Americus Reed II, marketing professor at the Wharton School of Business, offers his own word of caution, using a vivid metaphor: "A focus group is like a chainsaw. If you know what you are doing, it's very useful and effective. If you don't, you could lose a limb."[9]

How does ethnographic marketing inform our understanding of how leaders can become more effective problem-finders? Asking your employees questions, holding town-hall meetings, talking to customers and suppliers—all these activities certainly provide senior leaders with useful information at times. You may discover key problems and identify competitive threats through these discussions. Courageous subordinates may bring forward some bad news, or blow the whistle on activities that could compromise the firm's reputation and image. However, leaders must proceed with caution. People will say one thing, yet do another. They often will not intend to deceive; they may not even realize that they act differently than they say. Worse yet, the gap between talk and behavior typically widens when individuals come together in group discussions. The presence and influence of others around us cause us to describe our behavior even more inaccurately than we normally do.

Firsthand observation may yield very different insights about the activities and behaviors of employees, customers, suppliers, competitors, and strategic partners. Simply talking with others may cause leaders to proceed down the wrong path. You may hear about problems that, in fact, do not pose much of a threat at all. Meanwhile, you may not hear about problems that could have a great impact on the organization. Watching how the organization actually functions can be a very powerful and illuminating learning experience—and a far more accurate one. Firsthand observation—a simple version of ethnography—must become part of every leader's toolkit. To serve as effective problem-finders, we need to "get out and look," as A. G. Lafley has noted.

Proctor & Gamble does not simply leave this observational work to its research professionals in the marketing department. The firm's executives have become ethnographers and anthropologists too. Senior leaders leave their offices and go out into the field regularly so that they can see the problems and product flaws that must be addressed to satisfy customer needs. Firsthand observation of people in their natural context has become a critical problem-finding tool at P&G. By discovering problems and needs proactively, the firm has driven product improvements and innovations that have led to robust revenue growth throughout this decade.

Proctor & Gamble makes firsthand observation a responsibility of each of its senior leaders. According to Thomas Kinder, a vice president responsible for innovation at the firm, all executives must go on two home visits and two shopping trips with customers each year.[10] These interactions take place around the globe. As Chairman of the Board and CEO, Lafley too takes part in these home visits and shopping trips with consumers. As *Forbes* magazine explained, "Like the monarch in Mark Twain's *A Connecticut Yankee in King Arthur's Court*, Lafley often makes house calls incognito to find out what's on the mind of his subjects."[11]

Kinder explains that he has learned a great deal watching people shop in various countries. He says that he gained a new perspective on consumer decision-making from these visits, insights he could not have gleaned from examining mounds of data back in his office in Cincinnati, Ohio. Kinder feels that these direct observations keep him connected to the marketplace far more than anything else he could do. He and other P&G executives spot problems and identify opportunities for improvement each time they venture into the field. Moreover, executives come to truly believe in the power of ethnographic research. Therefore, they more readily endorse the innovations that result from this anthropological work being done by their marketing experts.[12]

Why Don't People Do What They Say?

Why must leaders become astute observers to spot problems proactively, rather than simply asking questions and inviting comments? Let's delve deeper to understand why people say one thing and do another. Many reasons exist for this gap between statements and behavior—ranging from the behavior of the questioner to the workings of the unconscious mind.

Leading Questions

When speaking with colleagues or customers, we may pose questions that elicit the responses we would like to hear. The answers may not reflect what people actually believe or what is actually taking place in the organization. Let's face it—leaders often seek validation from their subordinates, more so than unvarnished advice. Sometimes, we simply word questions in a way that drives responses in a certain direction or that narrows the scope of dialogue that follows. We do so intentionally at times, and unknowingly on other occasions.

Psychologist Elizabeth Loftus has done influential research on the subject of leading questions—specifically, how small changes in wording make a big difference. In one study, she showed a group of students a video of an automobile accident in which one driver runs through a stop sign, turning right into busy traffic and causing a five-car collision. After showing the video, she distributed a survey to the students. She asked half the students, "How fast was Car A going when it ran the stop sign?" She asked the other half, "How fast was Car A going when it turned right?" Loftus then asked everyone, "Did you see a stop sign for Car A?" Fifty-three percent of the students in the first group answered that they had seen the stop sign, yet only 35% of the students in the second group indicated that they had noticed it. Loftus concludes that we can affect responses by including or excluding crucial presuppositions in our questions. She defines a presupposition as "a condition that must hold in order for the question to be contextually appropriate." In this case, one question presupposes the existence of the stop sign.[13]

In a subsequent experiment, Loftus shows how even false presuppositions can distort responses. She again showed a video of an automobile accident. This time, she asked half the students, "How fast was the white sports car going when it passed the barn while traveling along the country road?" In fact, the video showed no barn along the street. The other half received the same question, except without mention of the barn. Loftus then asked all the students, "Did you see a barn?" Roughly six times as many students in the first group than in the second indicated that they had seen a barn in the video. Insertion of the false presupposition had distorted people's recall and response.[14]

Many of us include presuppositions in our questions at times, and thus we may word our questions in ways that may distort the responses we receive. Presuppositions do not have to be as blatant as those in Professor Loftus' research. They often come in the form of a taken-for-granted assumption that we insert into questions. For instance, an executive might ask, "How much will revenue rise if we cut prices?" The executive not only has assumed that consumers will buy more products when prices fall, but that the increased volume will more than compensate for the decreased revenue per unit.

In many cases, leading questions come in the form of a request for an endorsement of a particular course of action. One might say, "Do you agree that we should make this acquisition?" Or, you might be even more forceful: "You agree with this acquisition, don't you?" That wording certainly does not invite a wide-ranging discussion of divergent perspectives; in fact, it seems to actively discourage the expression of dissenting views. The respondent may have crucial information about the pitfalls of this acquisition, or the problems currently taking place at the target firm, but these issues are less likely to surface given the form of the question.

Group Dynamics

Leaders often solicit feedback from others in groups, both large and small. They attend meetings, hold town-hall forums, and perhaps host lunches with groups of employees. They interact with teams of people when they visit customers and suppliers as well. Unfortunately, group dynamics often cause people to say things that may not reflect how they actually behave. How does being in a group setting distort people's responses to a leader's inquiries?

First, a few loud voices, or perhaps a table-thumper or two, certainly can easily quash the level of candid discussion within a group. These individuals can dominate the airtime, making it difficult for others to join the discussion. A vociferous individual may cause the conversation to focus narrowly on his or her preferred topic, and combativeness may lead to some uncomfortable tension with senior leaders in the room. That tension can certainly quiet a room in a hurry.

Second, individuals may not want to disclose their preferences or opinions in front of others. That hesitancy may be most pronounced if they do not have close relationships with the others in that forum. For instance, marketers find that focus group participants sometimes feel reluctant to disclose their tastes, needs, and desires in front of strangers. The lack of interpersonal trust drives a wedge between what people say and their actual behavior. At a forum, such as a town-hall meeting, employees may face similar concerns. They may be together with people in other units of the organization, with whom they have not worked closely. The room also may contain managers from multiple levels of the hierarchy, including the direct supervisors of frontline employees. Thus, people may not speak freely when invited to do so by senior leaders.

Finally, marketers have learned that individuals distort their true preferences in some cases because they are concerned about how they are presenting themselves to others. People worry about whether their views will be considered socially acceptable, and they try to portray a certain image to others in the group. For instance, a consumer may not disclose that she smokes if she senses that others in a group disapprove of cigarettes. Marketers found a particularly striking result with regard to advertisements that disparage competitors. In focus groups, individuals often do not admit to enjoying these ads, while in fact, research shows that these types of pitches are very effective.[15]

The Unconscious Mind

People often say one thing when confronted with an abstract idea and then act in a different manner when that idea becomes a reality for them. Marketers, for instance, find that individuals sometimes offer inaccurate responses because they do not have experience using a particular product or service. Seeing it for the first time in a focus group, they offer an immediate reaction as to whether they might purchase the item. Yet they may not actually choose the product once they become more familiar with it. Robbie Blinkoff, a managing partner at Context-Based Research Group, explains: "When you ask somebody a question, they'll have an opinion, and they may know absolutely nothing about it, or have never experienced it. It's abstracted from their reality."[16] Similarly, employees, suppliers, or strategic partners may offer feedback when presented with a new idea, but at that moment, it might still be a rather intangible and theoretical concept. Their reactions may change when they have actually garnered hands-on experience with the work associated with that proposed course of action.

Gerald Zaltman's research similarly suggests that the discrepancy between saying and doing may be completely unintentional. He points to the role of the unconscious mind in driving our actions. Put simply, Zaltman has concluded that customers may not always be able to discern what they want: "Unconscious thoughts are the most accurate predictors of what people will actually do. In the space of five or ten minutes in a focus group, which is the average airtime per person, you can't possibly get at one person's unconscious thinking."[17] Employees, suppliers, and other constituents might have a similar problem when asked to react to a proposal from a firm's leaders. They may not recognize how their unconscious thoughts and feelings will compel them to act when that proposal becomes a reality in the organization.

Organizational learning experts Chris Argyris and Donald Schon also conclude that the unconscious mind plays a role in explaining the gap between what people say and do. They argue that we have certain mental models, or theories, in our heads that govern how we will act in certain circumstances. Argyris and Schon explain that we actually hold two separate "theories of action" in our brains:

> "When someone is asked how he would behave under certain circumstances, the answer he usually gives is his espoused theory of action for that situation. This is the theory of action to which he gives allegiance, and which, upon request, he communicates to others. However, the theory that actually governs his actions is his theory-in-use."[18]

To give an example, our espoused theory might be that we should bring difficult issues out in the open when tensions arise at work, and then collaborate to resolve these differences constructively. However, our theory-in-use often involves a set of behaviors intended to avoid embarrassment and confrontation. Argyris and Schon describe these behaviors as defensive routines, which often characterize our theories-in-use. Why does this gap between theories-in-use and espoused theories persist over time? Argyris and Schon argue that individuals typically do not recognize the theories-in-use that govern their actions. Moreover, we remain oblivious to the schism between our espoused theories and theories-in-use. The gap between what we say and what we do stubbornly endures for these reasons.[19]

Honing Your Powers of Observation

Now you understand that discovering your organization's problems requires more than a few town-hall meetings to ask for employee input. Effective leaders become adept at watching how customers shop, employees work, and competitors behave. They break out of the isolation of the executive suite and "get out and look." They do not simply "manage by walking around." They become careful and systematic observers of people, processes, and facilities. They immerse themselves in the everyday contexts in which work is being done and in which consumers buy and use their products. They engage with people on the front lines of organizations, and they get their hands dirty doing some of the real work that must be done to serve customers. Working alongside their employees, they see how things actually get done.

Take David Neeleman, the founder of JetBlue. Neeleman launched a quite successful new airline in an era when most airlines have suffered financial ruin. More recently, he's moved on to launch an airline startup in Brazil. JetBlue not only generated profits in most years of his tenure as CEO, but it also scored very highly on the airline quality rankings (AQR)—a scoring system that measures everything from on-time arrivals to mishandled baggage and customer complaints. In fact, from 2003 to 2007, JetBlue ranked number one or number two each year on the AQR, even though it experienced an embarrassing week of travel delays in February 2007. The company's rapid recovery from those troubles enabled it to maintain its high ranking for the year overall.[20]

How did Neeleman create such a customer-friendly airline? How did he deliver on his promise of exceptional service? One reason may be that he chose to work alongside his frontline employees, and interact directly with his customers, on a regular basis. He never allowed himself to become too distant from the basic process of helping customers enjoy their flights. How did he do it? While on board one of his planes, Neeleman would introduce himself to the passengers over the intercom. Then he would join his flight attendants in providing drink and snack service, in what one journalist described as his "snack and schmooze drill." Neeleman actually donned an apron with his nickname—"Snack Boy"—as he worked the aisles.[21] Neeleman not only had an opportunity to listen to and observe customers on these occasions, but he also interacted closely with his pilots and flight attendants. He could see them in action and speak with them very informally. One crew member explained, "Seeing David is great. He's so easygoing, and we get to talk."[22]

How do leaders become astute observers when they venture out of their offices? For starters, you might adhere to some of the very same principles and techniques used by expert ethnographers (summarized in Table 3.1).[23] First, make a firm decision about whether you intend to become a participant-observer. Do you intend to work the aisles, like David Neeleman, or will you sit back and watch? In some cases, you will want to become a participant in the action. At other times, it may be more helpful to remain unobtrusive, perhaps even trying to avoid being noticed.

TABLE 3.1   Principles of Effective Observation

Do's	Don'ts
Try to wipe away preconceived notions before starting your observations.	Begin with a strong expectation of what you expect to see.
Collect observations under different circumstances and from varied perspectives.	Draw major conclusions from a very small and/or biased sample of observations.
Seek informants wisely.	Rely on the lone voice of a so-called expert.
Take good notes, including quotes from key conversations, and collect important artifacts.	Try to commit everything strictly to memory.
Engage in active listening.	Ask leading questions.
Keep systematic track of observations that surprise you or contradict your prior beliefs.	Seek and record data primarily to prove a preexisting hypothesis.

Disavow yourself of any preconceived notions about your organization or its employees, customers, or competitors. You have to try to wipe the slate clean, no matter how hard that may be. Be careful about even having a precise view of what you are setting out to learn. As Siamack Salari, a marketing research expert, points out, "Ethnographic research is always agenda-less. It's totally opposed to other forms of research and its big benefit is that it generates insights. It uncovers things you didn't know you didn't know about."[24]

Practice a technique that researchers call "triangulation."[25] Collect multiple observations from different vantage points. Do not rely simply on what you see; collect artifacts from your visits—whether that be a flyer from the factory bulletin board, one of your competitor's brochures, or a sign that a local manager created to welcome new shoppers to your stores. Consider bringing along your digital camera, or taking a few photos with your cell phone, if you see something interesting. You may never be able to capture a thought in writing as well as you can by taking a photograph.

Seek out informants wisely. You will often, but not always, do more than observe as you venture into the field; you will speak with a variety of people, often rather informally. Search for the individuals who are most willing to open up to you, to be candid. In many cases, certain people have developed a reputation inside the firm for being straight shooters. Seek them out. Recognize, though, that each person has a limited perspective from his or her own vantage point. Thus, do not rely on a few voices. Speak to people in their own language. In other words, recognize that the way in which you talk with your engineers should be quite different from the conversation you may have with your salespeople. Try to learn the terminology of a local unit, and then speak with them using that vocabulary.[26]

As you speak with individuals, employ open-ended inquiries, and try to avoid leading questions. Engage in active listening, meaning that you should periodically play back what you are hearing, asking for validation and clarification of your interpretations. Finally, as you take notes, try to record key quotes from your conversations. Keeping track of what you have heard in your employees' and customers' own words can be very powerful. Sharing those direct quotes with other executives has tremendous persuasive power.

Throughout these conversations, remember to spend much more time listening than talking. The more airtime you consume, the less opportunity others have to inform you. Speaking precludes learning at times. As one researcher at Ogilvy and Mather, the renowned advertising agency, noted after a trip to study women consuming shampoo in Thai villages: "I learned that if you really want to know what's going on around you, you just have to shut up and listen."[27]

Finally, keep track of what you are observing. Take careful notes, and as you do, make a clear distinction between fact and interpretation. You should jot down your feelings and impressions about various situations, but be sure to distinguish those subjective judgments from the factual evidence. Seek out, and systematically track, the things that surprise or confuse you. As organizational learning expert David Garvin argues, the best observers seek out "anomalies, exceptions, and contradictory evidence." He points out that Charles Darwin "went so far as to keep a separate record of all observations that contradicted his theory."[28]

When you are done with your observations, you should find some time to synthesize what you have learned. If you have partnered with another observer, spend time comparing notes. Explore the differences in your observations and interpretations, and inquire as to why you viewed the same situations quite differently. Finally, develop a concrete list of the problems you spotted and the opportunities for improvement. Then, bounce these ideas off others who did not take part in the observations, to see how they react to what you have learned. Ask them what else they would like to know, and consider what new information-gathering you would like to conduct before moving forward.[29]

A Few Words of Caution

Tom Stemberg, the founder of Staples, believes fervently in the power of firsthand observation and immersive experiences.[30] When he served as Staples' CEO, all new employees, regardless of their position in the organizational hierarchy, spent their first few days at the company working in a retail store. They would stock shelves, operate a cash register, unload incoming shipments, and assist shoppers. Even the most senior hires took part in these activities in their first few weeks at the company. Stemberg also spent a great deal of time in the chain's stores, and he perused his competitors' locations on a regular basis. Beyond that, Stemberg took time to observe retailers that did not compete with Staples; he loved learning from Costco, for example. He even spent time visiting firms in other industries. For instance, he once set out to learn about customer service at Mobil, focusing on its Speed Pass Program, which was relatively new at the time.

Stemberg points out one key problem with these visits. When people learned that he was coming, they would alter their behavior. Ethnographers fret over the same problem when they conduct their research. They recognize that their mere presence may distort the subjects' behavior. Stemberg recounts one such instance:

> "This week I was in Pittsburgh and Youngstown, Ohio...When I walked into the next store, in New Kensington, PA, three people approached me. It was too good to be true. I said, 'I've got a funny feeling you were waiting for me.' The manager there said, 'Well, I guess we were. We heard you were coming.' I said, 'I guess the guy in Youngstown must have called you.' He said, 'Yeah, he did, but he didn't have to—the word was out last night when you got to Uniontown.'"[31]

The observer's influence on others' behavior constitutes a thorny challenge, particularly for a senior executive. People certainly do not act the same way when the boss enters the room. How can leaders deal with this challenge? First, the leader does not have to reveal his or her identity when interacting with certain constituents, such as customers. Individuals should not lie, but they could simply state that they work for the company, without making a big deal of the fact that they actually are one of the top executives at the firm. Second, leaders may use others who are less well known throughout the organization to conduct similar observations, and then spend time comparing notes. That method may be particularly useful when observing internal company operations. The second set of eyes may provide some illuminating insights, if indeed the senior leader's presence distorted others' behavior.

Stemberg tells a funny story about the use of another set of eyes. He once asked his mother-in-law to order, and then return, office supplies from the delivery arm of one of his rivals! As a result, he learned a great deal about his competitor's return policies and procedures.[32] Third, leaders can actually take part in the work on the front lines, as Neeleman did at JetBlue. By becoming a participant-observer, Neeleman experienced key activities and interactions for himself. He did not rely strictly on the observations of others. Neeleman made the practice of donning the apron rather commonplace; when such activity becomes routine, the likelihood of distorted behavior declines. He built a rapport with the crew members on the company's planes as he worked the aisles so that over time, they came to trust him and become more open with him about problems that needed to be addressed. Finally, leaders can check the conclusions from their observations against other data. For instance, did a store visit yield an experience consistent with customer satisfaction surveys for that location? If inconsistencies emerge from that comparison, leaders can sit down with employees to discuss the discrepancies.

This chapter closes with a final word of caution about moving into the field to conduct firsthand observations. Our minds can play games with us. We can convince ourselves that we do not have anything to learn from others. Our existing mental models may prove so strong that we cannot acknowledge or accept a discordant perspective. For instance, our customers may be using our products in an unintended fashion. Their behavior may represent a remarkable revenue growth opportunity, yet we may dismiss the behavior as odd or misinformed. Take, for example, the famous case of Kleenex tissues. The creators originally intended for this product to be used to help women remove their makeup. As it turned out, many men chose to use Kleenex tissues to blow their noses. When executives learned about this behavior, they shrugged it off initially. It took quite some time for managers to accept this alternative use and integrate it into their marketing campaigns.[33]

Stemberg tells a startling story about the failure to be open to all learning possibilities when observing the competition. Here's his story:

> "Back in 1987 one of the founders of Office Depot was dying. It was tragic. Some venture capitalist was trying to buy the company very cheaply and put in a new CEO. Some of the incumbent investors, many of whom we knew, said to us, 'Why don't you just come in and buy this?' At that time, we could have bought Office Depot for $12 million or $14 million. And so to get an assessment of how the company was doing—we hadn't been there in awhile—we sent two people down. They rented a convertible and drove around for two days to all the stores, and they reported back that essentially there was no sense in buying those guys because they would be gone by the end of the year: they were so bad, the service was no good, nothing was right. Well, of course, Office Depot has gone on to become the biggest company in the industry."[34]

Stemberg recounts a lesson that he learned from Wal-Mart founder Sam Walton about how to derive value from every observation. The legendary merchant loved to scout his competition, and he required his employees to do the same. Walton, though, "would force you to focus on what they did better than you did."[35] He would not allow people to dismiss their observations and rationalize away possible problems that might exist back at Wal-Mart. Walton could find the smallest thing that a rival did better than his firm, even at the most poorly run companies. Put simply, you can spot problems through observation only if you begin by acknowledging that problems always exist, even at the best-run companies. One can always improve. Without that mindset, all the effort of firsthand observation may be futile.

Endnotes

[1] Horovitz, B. "Marketers take a close look at your daily routine." *USA Today*, April 29, 2007.

[2] Ibid.

[3] Kroll, L. "A fresh face." *Forbes*. July 8, 2002.

[4] Lafley, A. G. and R. Charan. (2008). *The Game-Changer: How You Can Drive Revenue and Profit Growth with Innovation*. New York: Crown Business. p. 49. The authors do a very nice job of describing how Proctor & Gamble jump-started innovation and organic revenue growth during Lafley's tenure. Lafley describes many of the key initiatives, including Workin' It and Livin' It.

[5] Horovitz, B. (2007).

[6] Mead, M. (1928). *Coming of Age in Samoa*. New York: Morrow Quill.

[7] One of the most accomplished organizational ethnographers is John Van Maanen of the Sloan School of Management at the Massachusetts Institute of Technology. He wrote a superb book about ethnographic research methods in the 1980s. See Van Maanen, J. (1988). *Tales of the Field on Writing Ethnography*. Chicago: University of Chicago Press.

[8] Gross, D. "Lies, damn lies, and focus groups." *Slate*. October 10, 2003. For more on Zaltman's research, see Zaltman, G. (2003). *How Customers Think: Essential Insights into the Mind of the Market*. Boston: Harvard Business School Press.

[9] Tischler, L. (2007). "Every move you make." *Fast Company*.

[10] Interview with Thomas Kinder, Vice President—Global Market Strategy and Planning, Proctor & Gamble Corporation. I met Mr. Kinder when we each presented at a Bord Bia conference in Ireland (Bord Bia is the Irish Food Agency) in May 2008. Tom and I had the pleasure of talking about Proctor & Gamble's ethnographic research initiatives over a few Guinness draughts at Johnnie Fox's pub, located in Glencullen on top of the Dublin mountains—certainly one of the best interview locations I can recall!

[11] Kroll, L. (2002).

[12] For more on ethnographic marketing, see Mariampolski, H. (2005). *Ethnography for Marketers: A Guide to Consumer Immersion*. Thousand Oaks, CA: Sage Publications.

[13] Loftus, E. (1975). "Leading questions and the eyewitness report." *Cognitive Psychology*. 7: 550–572. For more on the remarkable and impactful research of Stanford psychologist Elizabeth Loftus, see Garry, M. and H. Hayne. (2006). *Do Justice and Let the Sky Fall: Elizabeth F. Loftus and Her Contributions to Science, Law, and Academic Freedom*. Philadelphia: Lawrence Erlbaum.

[14] Loftus, E. (1975).

[15] Gross, D. (2003). See also Rubin, H. and I. Rubin. (2004). *Qualitative Interviewing: The Art of Hearing Data*. Thousand Oaks, CA: Sage Publications.

[16] Gross, D. (2003).

[17] Ibid.

[18] Argyris, C. and D. Schon. (1981). *Theory in Practice: Increasing Professional Effectiveness*. San Francisco: Jossey-Bass. p. 7.

[19] Ibid.

[20] Bowen, B. and D. Hadley. (2007). *Airline Quality Rankings*. http://aqr.aero/aqrreports/AQR2007full.pdf. Bowen and Hadley publish these airline quality rankings annually. Their methodology is quite thorough, and it provides a fascinating look at the state of a very troubled industry.

[21] Peterson, B. (2004). *Blue Streak: Inside JetBlue, the Upstart That Rocked an Industry*. New York: Penguin Books.

[22] Newman, R. (2004). "Preaching JetBlue: How David Neeleman is spreading the gospel of service at the fast-growing airline." *The Chief Executive*. October issue.

[23] For a useful description of ethnographic research methods, see Genzuk, M. (2003). "A Synthesis of Ethnographic Research." *Occasional Papers Series, Center for Multilingual Research*. University of Southern California, Rossier School of Education.

[24] Hoare, S. "Big brands turning to Big Brother." *The Daily Telegraph*. March 29, 2007.

[25] Yin, R. (1994). *Case Study Research: Design and Methods*. 2nd edition. Thousand Oaks, CA: Sage Publications.

[26] Understanding the language of an organization is critical, particularly for a new leader who comes from the outside. Robert Nardelli learned this the hard way when he arrived at The Home Depot after many years at General Electric. Unfamiliar with retailing, he made some significant language gaffes in his first few months at the Atlanta home improvement retailer. For instance, he referred to the merchandising organization as the "purchasing group"—a term not looked upon kindly by retail merchants. He also referred to stock-keeping units as "S.K.U.s" rather than "skus"—the term used throughout the retail sector. See Sellers, P. "Home Depot: Exit the builder, enter the repairman." *Fortune*. March 29, 2001.

[27] Tischler, L. (2007).

[28] Garvin, D. (2000). *Learning in Action: A Guide to Putting the Learning Organization to Work*. Boston: Harvard Business School Press. pp. 79–80.

[29] IDEO, the leading product-design firm, practices many of the principles of effective observation as it conducts the research required to develop innovative new products. For a wonderful demonstration of the IDEO product-development process in action, see the ABC News *Nightline* video titled "The Deep Dive," which aired July 13, 1999. In that program, hosted by Ted Koppel, ABC News chronicles IDEO's attempts to design a new supermarket shopping cart in just five days. The video provides a remarkable inside look at this highly creative firm. You actually get to see the entire product-development process unfold, from research and brainstorming to the creation of a fully functioning prototype that the designers

take to a store to gather feedback. One of the cofounders has written a very good book about innovation at IDEO. See Kelley, T. (2001). *The Art of Innovation: Lessons in Creativity from IDEO, America's Leading Design Firm*. New York: Doubleday. Several Harvard case studies also have been written about the firm. See Thomke, S. and A. Nimgade. (2000). "IDEO Product Development." Harvard Business School Case Study No. 9-600-143; Edmondson, A. and L. Feldman. (2005). "Phase Zero: Introducing New Services at IDEO (A)." Harvard Business School Case Study No. 9-605-069.

[30] This section draws upon an article in *Inc.* magazine. See Gruner, S. (1998). "Spies like us." *Inc.* magazine. August issue. It also draws upon my personal experience working at Staples from 1994 to 1996, when Tom Stemberg served as CEO. I had the opportunity to interact with Stemberg on a number of occasions during that time, and I learned a great deal about how he and others studied and analyzed the competition. At that time, Staples believed that every new employee, regardless of whether he was a store associate or senior executive, should begin his employment at the firm by working on the floor of a retail store. Thus, I spent my first week at the firm, after graduating with my MBA from Harvard, stocking shelves, answering shoppers' questions, and running a cash register at a Staples store in New London, Connecticut. I learned a great deal about Staples' customers and the store operations from the immersive experience.

[31] Gruner, S. (1998).

[32] Ibid.

[33] Sawyer, K. (2007). *Group Genius: The Creative Power of Collaboration*. New York: Perseus Books Group.

[34] Gruner, S. (1998).

[35] Ibid.

4

Hunt for Patterns

"To understand is to perceive patterns."
—Isaiah Berlin, political philosopher

In our research on Rapid Response Teams, we spoke with many nurses. We asked them to explain how they recognized the early warning signs of a patient headed for distress. In short, we wanted to know how they became effective problem-finders. Did it simply involve continuous monitoring of vital signs, with calls for assistance initiated when key metrics moved outside acceptable ranges? Time and time again, we heard that highly experienced nurses spotted trouble *before* the patient's vital signs became abnormal. In one hospital, we heard that more than 20% of recent Rapid Response Team calls originated with a nurse who requested assistance because "something just did not feel right." In contrast, novices often did not notice a problem until the quantitative measures moved outside the acceptable range. By then, a patient's condition might be quite serious.

We probed to find how the experienced nurses often recognized trouble unfolding at its early stages. What caused them to become concerned? One nurse said to us, "You just have a sense...I can't tell you exactly how that happens, but you somehow put two and two together. You look at the lab values and the patient, and you get a picture of what is going on. Sometimes it's just a sixth sense. I can't explain it!" Another nurse commented, "I've been a nurse for twenty-two years. You develop instincts about patient behavior and appearance. You can just look at an individual and say 'Uh-oh!' It might be their skin tone, or the way someone is talking. Ninety percent of the time, our gut is right. Sometimes, you can't quite put a finger on it, but you *know* the patient is crashing." We heard similar comments from nurses on countless occasions during our study.

Did this mean that novices could not become superb problem-finders until they had accumulated decades of experience? No, we discovered that the Rapid Response Team process could accelerate the inexperienced nurses' ability to spot trouble brewing in its infancy. Nurses kept telling us that calling a Rapid Response Team for assistance not only helped the patient, but it also sharpened their instincts. They learned from watching how and why their more experienced peers decided to call an RRT even when they lacked concrete data to support their concerns. Moreover, they learned by observing and interacting with the experts on the Rapid Response Teams. The novices watched how the RRT members assessed patients. What tests did they conduct? What questions did they ask? How did they draw conclusions based on limited data? How did they make links back to past cases?

The RRT members viewed each call as a "teaching moment" in which they could assist the patient *and* mentor the inexperienced nurses. The RRT members often asked the inexperienced nurses a series of questions about the patient's behavior and appearance over the previous few hours. They commented on signs of trouble that the novice might have missed. They "thought out loud" as they assessed the patient so that the novices could understand their thinking. Over time, the novices became more adept at noticing subtle signals of oncoming patient distress. As one RRT member said, "the program helps develop a new nurse's sixth sense." In short, intuition seemed to be a key problem-finding capability at these hospitals. However, good instincts were not purely an accident of birth. One could not conclude that some individuals simply were more fortunate, or more intelligent, and thus had better instincts than others. In fact, it appeared quite possible for experts to help others hone their intuition, thereby enabling them to become better problem-finders.

What Is Intuition?

A sixth sense, gut instinct, intuition...We all have experienced this phenomenon, but what precisely does it mean? How does the intuitive process work? Can we actually harness and enhance our intuition so as to become better problem-finders?

In 1985 psychologist Gary Klein set out to study how firefighters made life-or-death decisions.[1] In the process, he learned (unexpectedly) about the intuitive process. In his very first interview, Klein asked a fire commander to describe a very challenging incident in which he had been involved. The commander insisted that "ESP" had been a critical factor in making a good decision. Extrasensory perception? Was the commander kidding? The commander explained how he had once arrived at the scene of a seemingly small and straightforward kitchen fire. His men began spraying water at the fire from the living room, but "the fire just roared back at them."[2] After a few repeated attempts, the commander was puzzled. Why wasn't the water effective in fighting the fire? Then, his "sixth sense" kicked in, and he became very concerned. He ordered his men out of the house, despite not knowing precisely why the alarm bells had gone off in his head. Soon thereafter, the living room floor collapsed. If the firefighters had remained in the house, they could have been seriously injured or killed.

As Klein asked probing questions, the commander described what he was thinking at the time of the fire. He recalled being surprised that the water had virtually no impact on the fire. He remembered being puzzled by how hot it was in the living room. A small kitchen fire should not have emitted that much heat. Meanwhile, he heard very little noise when he was standing in the living room. That seemed odd, given that a hot fire such as this one should have been rather noisy. As it turned out, the floor collapsed because the main fire was located in the basement, directly beneath where he had been standing. That explained the ineffectiveness of the water, the extreme heat, and the low noise level. The commander did not know that at the time, but he *knew* that the situation didn't feel quite right. His intuition had helped him detect a serious problem. Klein explained his interpretation of the commander's thought process:

> "The whole pattern did not fit right. His expectations were violated, and he realized that he did not quite know what was going on. That was why he ordered his men out of the building...The commander's experience had provided him with a firm set of patterns. He was accustomed to sizing up a situation by having it match one of those patterns. He may not have been able to articulate the patterns or describe their features, but he was relying on the pattern-matching process to let him feel comfortable that he had the situation scoped out."[3]

Over time, Klein studied the decision-making of a variety of experts in other fields, including pilots, military leaders, and nurses. He concluded that intuition plays a powerful role in how experts size up a situation and make decisions. According to Klein, intuition is fundamentally a pattern-recognition process. When individuals encounter a situation, they try to determine whether it fits (or does not fit) the patterns of their past experience. That pattern-recognition process often involves drawing analogies between the current situation and past situations. The pattern-recognition activity then triggers a set of "action scripts" that enable individuals to decide and act without going through an elaborate comparison of multiple alternatives. Instead, they consider a potential plan of action, and they mentally simulate whether that plan might be effective. If so, they act. If not, they consider a different scenario/option.[4]

Klein argues that intuition gradually develops as someone develops deep expertise in a specific field. As an individual encounters more and more situations, he or she develops a more sophisticated ability to identify and match patterns. In other words, although we are not always aware of it, the mind hunts for patterns in all the situations that we encounter, and it uses pattern-matching to spot problems. Going back to the commander in our example, we see that he could not match the kitchen fire with the patterns from his past experience. He had seen many kitchen fires, and based on that experience, he expected to see certain patterns in terms of the noise level, the heat, and how water affected the fire. However, in this case, the cues that he observed did not match those patterns. Thus, his intuition told him that he was not experiencing a simple contained kitchen fire. He could not rely on the actions that he would have automatically and instinctively embarked upon if the situation matched the pattern of past kitchen fires. The lack of a pattern match led him to conclude that he might be facing a much more serious problem than he first envisioned.[5]

Faulty Analogies

As you learned from the firefighting example, the intuitive process rests firmly on our ability to draw appropriate analogies. Our minds appear to constantly ask the question: To what past circumstance is this current situation analogous? As it turns out, we use analogies to make decisions all the time. Sometimes, we do so unconsciously, and in other cases, we draw an analogy to a past situation in a much more open and deliberate fashion. Unfortunately, we sometimes draw inappropriate analogies, or we arrive at erroneous conclusions based on the analogies we make. Our search for patterns leads us astray. As a result, we do a poor job of detecting problems. We overestimate some and miss others.

Richard Neustadt and Ernest May have conducted groundbreaking research on the misuse of analogies.[6] They studied the American presidency and discovered a number of examples of faulty reasoning by analogy. Take, for example, the 1976 "swine flu" incident. In that situation, President Gerald Ford and his advisors drew an erroneous analogy to the infamous flu epidemic of 1918. The faulty analogy led them to dramatically overestimate the seriousness of the problem they faced. As a result, they embarked on a very expensive and unnecessary immunization program. Roughly five hundred people experienced a serious side effect that was linked to the immunizations, and twenty-five people died. The settlements cost the federal government millions of dollars. More people died from the immunizations than from the flu itself. The credibility of public-health authorities, as well as the Ford administration, took a major hit.

The incident began with a report that a soldier at Fort Dix had died from the flu, and several other soldiers became ill. The virus appeared to be chemically related to one that commonly affected pigs but that had not afflicted humans since the 1930s. However, experts believed that the 1930s virus represented a weaker version of a virus that caused a massive epidemic in 1918. In that year, a powerful and virulent influenza killed 500,000 Americans and roughly twenty million people around the globe. Many young adults in their prime died suddenly from this flu, apparently within a day or two of being diagnosed.

When the soldier died at Fort Dix, people drew an analogy to the 1918 epidemic. In part, they did so because of the biological link to the virus that caused so many deaths back then. Experts did not believe that the current virus that had killed the soldier at Fort Dix was as dangerous, but they could not be sure. Given the uncertainty, people made judgments based on their vivid memories of the stories they had heard from their parents about the horrendous epidemic of 1918. As Neustadt and May write, "it seems that almost everyone at higher levels of the federal government in 1976 had a parent, uncle, aunt, cousin, or at least a family friend who had told lurid tales of personal experience with the 1918 flu."[7]

Added pressure arose because Centers for Disease Control (CDC) officials did not want to repeat the experiences of 1957 and 1968. In those years, flu epidemics (unrelated to the 1918 virus) had caught the federal government off guard. Experts had come to believe that major shifts in influenza viruses took place roughly every decade; they worried that the death of this soldier might indicate the onset of another dangerous shift. Officials at the CDC wanted to demonstrate that they could move proactively to head off another epidemic; they wanted to show the country that they could do better than they had in 1968.

Over the course of ten weeks, forty million people received immunizations. However, a number of delays and public-relations blunders took place. Moreover, not a single person died anywhere in the world from swine flu, unless they had been in close contact with pigs. Meanwhile, roughly five hundred people contracted Guillain-Barré syndrome, apparently due to the vaccine. The disease can cause paralysis, and in the case of twenty-five individuals, it led to death due to respiratory problems. Because no one had contracted swine flu since the soldiers at Fort Dix had become ill, the government suspended the vaccination program. The initiative cost the government $137 million, plus millions more to settle cases brought by the families of those afflicted with Guillain-Barré syndrome. Newspapers at the time described the immunization program as a "fiasco" and a "debacle."[8]

Neustadt and May concluded that the Ford administration and the CDC had fallen victim to a captivating analogy rooted in folk memories of a horrible tragedy nearly sixty years earlier. The scholars explain:

> "Literally, the analogy was not 'irresistible.' Its relevance was limited, its application arguable, and its guidance dubious on what to do. It served better as a warning light than as a beacon. Yet it precipitated action on the basis, solely, of 'worst-case' analysis without preparing to accommodate the likely case. Captivated, the decision-makers failed to hedge by light of the uncertainty."[9]

What lies at the heart of faulty reasoning by analogy? Neustadt and May argue that we tend to dwell on and overestimate the similarities between two situations that we deem analogous, and we ignore many of the fundamental differences. The Ford administration certainly did both.

When we reason by analogy, we make a number of assumptions. For instance, officials assumed that no serious side effects existed, and that one dose of the vaccine would suffice. Both assumptions proved incorrect. In fact, government officials committed three types of errors with regard to the assumptions they made. They failed to surface all their implicit assumptions, they confused facts with assumptions, and they failed to test and probe their assumptions carefully. We all exhibit these errors at times. Neustadt and May argue that government officials made at least seven key implicit assumptions during the swine flu incident, and every one of those assumptions "would turn out wrong in practice."[10] In sum, the Ford administration "found" a problem that did not truly exist, because they engaged in faulty reasoning by analogy. They hunted for a pattern, but they made the wrong match.[11]

Solutions in Search of Problems

Companies, too, draw poor analogies to their past experiences. Scholars Giovanni Gavetti and Jan Rivkin argue that business executives get in particular trouble when they start with "a solution seeking a problem."[12] In typical analogical reasoning, we search our past experience for analogies to a current situation we are trying to address. However, in some cases, executives begin with a solution they adore, perhaps a business model that has been successful for them. Then, they search for new problems to which they can apply that solution. They have a hammer in search of a nail. This type of problem-finding can be highly problematic.

Take Zoots, the dry cleaning business founded in 1998 by Staples CEO Tom Stemberg and Todd Krasnow, Staples' head of sales and marketing. It began with a great deal of promise, but it burned through a lot of cash and struggled to turn a profit. The company ultimately dissolved in early 2008, with the sale of stores and delivery routes to rivals. Two former managers acquired some of the firm's locations and the rights to the brand name.[13]

What happened? The strategy began with the founders drawing a number of analogies between the office supply business and the dry cleaning industry. Stemberg and Krasnow saw an opportunity to consolidate a highly fragmented industry, as they had done with tremendous success in office supplies. Witnessing the thousands of mom-and-pop operations around the country, they believed they could exploit economies of scale relative to these tiny independents. In office supplies, they had built their own distribution centers to serve stores in a hub-and-spoke logistics network. This turned out to be much more efficient than direct store delivery by multitudes of vendors, or distribution through independent wholesalers. It gave Staples a huge advantage over independent office supply stores. In dry cleaning, Stemberg and Krasnow envisioned a hub-and-spoke network with centralized cleaning facilities serving an array of stores in a geographic area. They believed they could achieve a cost advantage over the independent cleaners, while providing an array of more innovative services.[14]

As it turned out, the dry cleaning industry exhibited a number of profound differences compared to office supplies. As Zoots tried to grow, it encountered numerous operational problems. Efforts to operate centralized cleaning facilities led to quality problems, burdensome fixed costs, and difficulties dealing with wild swings in volume from day to day. At the heart of it, standardization and scale provided Staples with a competitive advantage in office supplies. Dry cleaning remained a business that was fundamentally about customization at the local level; thus, it was far less amenable to the exploitation of scale economies.[15] Bill Fisher, chief executive of the Drycleaning & Laundry Institute, explained the challenge for large chains in this industry: "Unlike fast-food chains that standardize all the food and cooking techniques, dry cleaners deal with thousands of different garments with unique issues on a daily basis."[16]

Other companies also have struggled with strategies born from the misuse of analogies. In the beer industry, Pete Slosberg achieved great success with the founding of his microbrewery brand—Pete's Wicked Ale. After selling his company, he searched for another industry to which he could apply the business model that had worked so well in craft brewing. Slosberg founded Cocoa Pete's Chocolate Adventures—a manufacturer of gourmet chocolates—in the spring of 2002. A Stanford case study explains how Slosberg ended up drawing an analogy between beer and chocolate:

> "To Slosberg and his advisors, the domestic chocolate industry seemed to represent a near-identical match to the beer industry of the 1980s in market dynamics and composition. When they compared the different brands of chocolate by price per pound, their research indicated that the domestic market was dominated by three companies (Hershey, Mars, and Nestle) producing less flavorful, mass-market products, just like the beer industry's three domestic players (Anheuser Busch, Coors, and Miller) produced mass-market, less flavorful beer. Their analysis pointed to a gap in the domestic market of higher quality gourmet chocolate where they could move in, just as Pete's Brewing Company targeted the gap in domestic super premium beer. Additionally, many chocolate makers, such as Guittard, had excess production capacity at their plants and would happily produce private label chocolates, much like the many breweries with excess capacity Pete's Brewing Company could have used to produce Pete's Wicked Ale in the mid-1980s."[17]

Of course, key differences existed between beer and chocolate. For instance, the target market for craft brews such as Pete's Wicked Ale consisted of males aged eighteen to thirty-four; the target market for premium chocolate tended to be wealthier, more educated females. Moreover, outsourcing production to chocolate makers with excess capacity proved to be very challenging. Chocolate manufacturing and product packaging, in general, turned out to be much more complex than craft brewing.[18] Now six years since its founding, Cocoa Pete's has not approached the success achieved by Pete's Brewing.

Finally, we have the infamous case of Enron. In the early 1990s, Jeffrey Skilling built a lucrative business trading natural gas. People became very excited about the potential of this concept. Gradually, Enron began to look for other markets to which it could apply the same business model. Ultimately, the firm tried to build trading businesses in industries as diverse as electric power, pulp and paper, trucking, and broadband.[19]

How did Enron choose to enter these disparate markets? It drew analogies between these industries and the natural gas market of the late 1980s. In fact, the company identified a list of key characteristics of the natural gas market. Executives described these attributes as "the template." They believed that they could apply their natural gas trading model to any industry that exhibited these characteristics, in other words, they could just transfer the template. Here are some examples of the attributes they considered: Was the product a fungible commodity that could be divided into indistinguishable units? Did it have a complex and unique logistics system? Were there many buyers and sellers who lacked market power? Could one create standard contracts and product offerings? Could the product be purchased and sold for varying periods of time? Could Enron create financial instruments to hedge risk associated with these commodities? Managers used this template to search for new business opportunities. At its heyday, Enron had hundreds of bright young people searching madly for the next business to which they could apply the natural gas model. Each talented young person sought the opportunity to pitch his or her idea to senior executives.[20]

What went wrong with this approach to new business creation? It encouraged managers at Enron to focus on the similarities between the natural gas market and these other industries as they drew analogies. However, it did not cause them to attend to the fundamental differences between markets. Many industries exhibited a majority of the attributes listed on Enron's "template." However, most industries also exhibited key differences that made establishing a profitable trading model quite difficult, particularly for an energy company without experience in that particular market. Going through the template did not require managers to think about those differences. It simply asked them to consider whether the similarities were present.

These examples—Zoots, Cocoa Pete's, and Enron—all demonstrate how vulnerable business leaders can be to faulty reasoning by analogy. Executives appear to be especially vulnerable when they have had great past success, like Krasnow at Staples, Slosberg at Pete's Brewing, and Skilling with the Enron gas trading business. We sometimes find ourselves starting with solutions in search of problems. As a result, we become even more likely to dwell on the similarities and discount the differences inherent in the analogy we have chosen. The lesson is simple: We can and should hunt for patterns all the time, but beware—we do not always make the right matches. Sometimes, we force matches where a pattern does not fit because we have a hammer in search of a nail.

Building Your Pattern-Recognition Capabilities

Let's turn now to how leaders can refine and enhance their pattern-recognition capabilities. We focus on how to reason more effectively by analogy, mentor inexperienced employees to help them spot problems sooner, and employ systematic analysis to spot patterns across your organization.

Better Analogies

Neustadt and May have proposed a simple methodology for enhancing our pattern-matching capabilities. They argue that leaders should begin by closely examining the current situation they face and then distinguishing what is *Known*, *Unclear*, and *Assumed*. Leaders cannot identify a useful analogy, or use it properly, if they do not have a clear grasp of the situation at hand. The exercise forces people to surface implicit assumptions and to separate assumption from fact. Seven questions can help you scrutinize your assumptions effectively (see Table 4.1).

TABLE 4.1   Scrutinizing Our Assumptions: Seven Key Questions

1. What are the facts in this situation?

2. What issues remain ambiguous or uncertain?

3. What explicit and implicit assumptions have we made?

4. Have we confused facts with assumptions?

5. How would an outsider with an unbiased perspective evaluate each of our assumptions?

6. How would our conclusions change if each of our key assumptions proves incorrect?

7. Can we collect data, conduct a simple experiment, or perform certain analysis to validate or disprove crucial assumptions?

Neustadt and May also suggest that leaders scrutinize their analogies closely, by drawing up two lists, *before* they try to determine how to act in the current situation. These lists should identify all the *Likenesses* and *Differences* between the current situation and the analogous one. Making people focus explicitly on the differences helps protect against becoming captivated by analogies that appear to match beautifully at first glance.

Leaders should try to write down these lists, "even if only on the back of an envelope."[21] The exercise of writing things down adds discipline and rigor to a leader's thought process. Moreover, it provides others an opportunity to offer more thoughtful criticism, after considerable reflection upon what they have read, rather than asking them to react quickly to statements bandied about in formal or informal meetings. Neustadt and May cite former Chrysler CEO Lee Iacocca's advice in this regard: "In conversation, you can get away with all kinds of vagueness and nonsense, often without realizing it. But there's something about putting your thoughts on paper that forces you to get down to specifics. That way, it's harder to deceive yourself—or anybody else."[22]

Neustadt and May explain how this methodology could have helped President Truman when he chose to go to war in Korea. At the time, Truman and his advisors relied on an analogy to the 1930s, when appeasement encouraged further aggression and ultimately led to World War II. The analogy has been used time and time again over the years, sometimes quite inappropriately. Truman explained his thinking about Korea in his memoirs:

> "I recalled some earlier instances: Manchuria, Ethiopia, Austria. I remembered how each time that the democracies failed to act it had encouraged the aggressors to keep going ahead. Communism was acting in Korea just as Hitler, Mussolini, and the Japanese had acted ten, fifteen, and twenty years earlier."[23]

Neustadt and May defend Truman's decision to come to the aid of South Korea. However, they point out that a disciplined examination of the 1930s analogy might have prevented one crucial error during the war—namely, the decision to allow General Douglas McArthur to push into North Korea in hopes of reunifying the nation after his initial success at driving the Communist troops out of the south. That decision, of course, ultimately led to the introduction of Chinese troops into the war. McArthur's troops were driven back, and the war's popularity at home plummeted.

Neustadt and May explain how a more careful analysis of the 1930s analogy might have prevented Truman from trying to reunify Korea. They argue that a comparison of *Likenesses* and *Differences* would have highlighted that "the President's chief concern was not Korea."[24] Instead, Truman wanted to deter further Soviet aggression and maintain the new postwar system of collective security. Careful examination of the analogies to the 1930s would have revealed that Truman wanted to use force to repel the aggressors, but not to "punish" or "seek retribution" against them for invading South Korea. After all, Truman and his advisors did not believe that the Allied forces should have "solved the Rhineland crisis by themselves occupying some portions of Germany" during the 1930s.[25] However, because the Truman administration did not fully vet the analogy, they allowed their original objective to drift from repelling the aggressors to reunifying the Korean peninsula. They discounted the possibility of Chinese entry into the war, because that dynamic was *fundamentally different* from anything they remembered from the 1930s.[26]

Mentoring

We can hone our pattern-recognition capability through interacting with experts in various fields, by digging in to understand their thought processes. How do they size up situations? How do they recognize problems and trends? What subtle signals serve as warnings to them? We also can foster mentoring relationships, whereby our internal experts can hone the pattern-recognition capacity of the less experienced members of our organizations.

The hospitals in our study coached the experts to mentor the novice nurses. As one hospital leader told us, "We wanted to mentor the more inexperienced nurses, and we wanted to help them develop their instincts, their ability to see when a patient might be deteriorating, even if the vitals looked OK." How did that mentoring take place? One hospital leader explained, "Often, the Rapid Response Team members will ask leading questions, sort of like the Socratic method. The idea is to take the floor nurse through a thought process... The mentoring, of course, comes later if the situation is a true crisis. Just act, and do the talking through the thought process later."

The experts pointed out that they sometimes needed to show restraint in order to share their intuition with less experienced colleagues. One nurse commented that, "It's straightforward for me to just act automatically. Sometimes, though, I do talk out loud about it as I'm doing something... Learning then is by osmosis." Experts feel tempted to just take over in many situations, but then the less experienced colleague may not understand *how* an expert arrived at certain conclusions. Communication of an expert's thought process becomes critical. One expert explained, "You just talk through your thought process at times, or the new nurse asks: 'How did you know?' Then, you can try to explain what you saw when you assessed the patient." Sometimes, that "talking out loud" occurs in real time; in other situations, it happens during a debriefing session after a situation has been resolved.

To help this learning take place, the hospitals find that it helps for the experts to show empathy for their inexperienced peers. They need to show the novices that they once walked in their shoes. They did not always possess the intuition to spot problems quickly and proactively. It took time to develop those instincts. One hospital leader explained:

> "We encourage the RRT to share a past experience, to show empathy with the floor nurse... 'I was scared when I first encountered this type of situation too...let me tell you about it.' We also want the RRT to share what they did in that past experience, what they thought it was, and how they might not have perceived a situation correctly when they first encountered it. In other words, show that they too were a novice once, and were surprised by something being different than they expected and unfamiliar to them."

Mentoring, then, requires astute observation and active listening on the part of the inexperienced, as well as empathy and communication skills on the part of the expert.[27] Most of all, learning simply occurs "by osmosis." As you talk through situations with others, and watch them handle those circumstances, you should keep asking yourself: What are they seeing that I am not seeing? How have they fit this situation into a pattern of their past experience? What cues are they attending in the current situation? As a leader, you can hone your own pattern-recognition capabilities, as well as encourage the experts in your organization to serve as mentors. The organization will benefit if everyone becomes better at recognizing patterns and spotting problems before they blossom into catastrophes.

Mining the Data

As small problems occur in your organization, consider how you catalog those incidents. Keeping careful track enables you to go back later and mine the data for patterns. Have we seen this type of problem repeatedly in various parts of the organization? What do these incidents have in common? Do we have a pattern here, suggesting a larger, more systemic problem?

At the hospitals, people track all the RRT calls. At one hospital, we observed a number of weekly review meetings that took place. A team of people sorted the data in many different ways. They asked questions such as: Does a particular unit seem to have a disproportionate number of incidents? Do we have a rash of calls associated with one particular "trigger" such as low oxygen saturation? Do the patients who require assistance have anything in common? At one weekly meeting, the team came to an important conclusion: Patients recovering from knee replacement surgery seemed to be experiencing a disproportionate number of RRT calls. Further analysis identified several factors contributing to this problem, and the team put in place several remedies to reduce the risk to these patients. In another hospital, similar review meetings revealed that the hospital had an over-sedation problem. Frequent RRT calls seemed to be occurring because patients experienced respiratory distress, as sometimes occurs with the use of sedatives. The hospital revised its policies for administering sedatives and monitoring those patients afterward so as to address the problem.

Other businesses can certainly mine data to hunt for patterns that reveal potentially serious problems within the organization. However, one can find patterns across multiple minor problems or incidents only if the data exist. In other words, transparency proves essential to pattern recognition. If the hospital did not know about the patients whose oxygen saturation had dropped unexpectedly, it would not have discovered its over-sedation problem. To see the patterns, people need to be willing to share their knowledge of situations that may not be transpiring as expected. They cannot fear the consequences of an organizational blame game.[28]

At PayPal, the highly profitable online payments unit of eBay, a unique process helps leaders spot patterns and identify problems before they mushroom. PayPal manager Mario Shiliashki described to me how each team within the company sends out a "PPP" (Progress, Problems, and Plans) report on a weekly basis.[29] The report identifies the team's progress on current initiatives, the problems it currently faces, and its plans to rectify those issues. The concise PPP report goes to a number of peer units, as well as to superiors within the organization. Shiliashki spends time each week reviewing the roughly ten to fifteen PPPs he receives. The transparency proves crucial to the company's continuous-improvement efforts. By examining a range of PPPs, each manager can see patterns across multiple units at PayPal. Are similar problems occurring in multiple units? Can teams collaborate to solve problems that they all face? Shiliashki explained that the PPP process "helps us get ahead of problems." In so doing, he finds that the process helps avoid the "blame game," because fewer "bad news surprises" occur. People hear about issues early, and they work collaboratively to solve them.

What Do You Learn at Business School?

Let's close this chapter with a thorny question: What precisely do individuals learn at business school, whether in MBA classrooms or Executive Education programs? Students surely ask themselves this question when they hand over hefty amounts of mney for tuition each year. Well, faculty members certainly teach a number of conceptual frameworks, and they expect the students to master them. Frequently, professors use case studies to help the students apply those frameworks to real managerial situations. Business education, though, involves far more than the learning of certain analytical techniques.

Beyond the frameworks, the case method of business education ultimately helps to hone an individual's pattern-recognition ability. Over the course of an MBA program, students see hundreds of scenarios through case studies. Clearly, the cases do not serve as pure substitutes for the real experience that experts achieve in the field. However, as students immerse themselves in these case situations, and compare and contrast them over time, they begin to recognize patterns. They draw analogies to past case studies. Thoughtful students begin to develop the capacity to discern when a situation fits patterns that they have seen repeatedly, and when it does not match prior patterns. In short, business education and leadership development programs offer the opportunity for leaders to become more adept at hunting for and spotting patterns.[30]

The promise of such learning experiences often falls short, though. Why? In part, too many case studies deprive students of the opportunity to work on their problem-finding skills. As former Secretary of Defense Robert McNamara (a Harvard Business School professor in the 1940s) once told me, case studies too often define the problem for the student.[31] They need only apply the right analytical technique to solve the problem. The best case studies make the students assess a situation, search for patterns, and *try to discern the problem for themselves.* Those types of cases provide enduring value, because they help build leaders' problem-finding capabilities—something they will desperately need in the "very messy" real world.

Endnotes

[1] Gary Klein has described his work in two excellent books. Klein, G. (1999). *Sources of Power: How People Make Decisions.* Cambridge, MA: MIT Press; Klein, G. (2004). *The Power of Intuition: How to Use Your Gut Feelings to Make Better Decisions at Work.* New York: Doubleday.

[2] Klein, (1999). p. 32.

[3] Ibid

[4] Daniel Isenberg has also done some excellent research on intuition—in particular, on how managers combine intuition and rational analysis. See Isenberg, D. (1984). "How senior managers think." *Harvard Business Review.* 62(6): 80–91.

[5] I have written several case studies that focus, in part, on the intuitive decision-making process. See Roberto, M. and G. Carioggia. (2004). "Electronic Arts: The Blockbuster Strategy." Harvard Business School Case Study No. 9-304-013; Roberto, M. and E. Ferlins (2004). "Fire at Mann Gulch." Harvard Business School Case Study No. 9-304-037; Roberto, M. and E. Ferlins (2005). "Storm King Mountain." Harvard Business School Case Study No. 9-304-046. In addition, Bryant University student Taryn Beaudoin recently completed her senior honors thesis under my supervision. She and I conducted extensive field research at GameWright, an award-winning games company located in Newton, Massachusetts. Her thesis is a case study of the firm. It focuses extensively on how managers at the firm employ intuition to make critical choices about which games to develop and produce. See Beaudoin, T. (2008). "Creativity, intuition, and product development: A case study of GameWright, Inc." Unpublished thesis. Smithfield, RI: Bryant University.

[6] Neustadt, R. and E. May. (1986). *Thinking in Time: The Uses of History for Decision-Makers.* New York: Free Press.

[7] Ibid, p. 49.

[8] For more on the swine flu incident, see Warner, J. "The Sky is Falling: An Analysis of the Swine Flu Affair of 1976." http://www.haverford.edu/biology/edwards/disease/viral_essays/warnervirus.htm.

[9] Neustadt, R. and E. May. (1986). p. 56.

[10] Neustadt, R. and E. May. (1986). p. 54.

[11] For faculty members interested in teaching a case study about the swine flu incident, see Neustadt, R. (1993). "Swine Flu Scare in America (A)." Harvard University John F. Kennedy School of Government Case Study No. KSG1053.0. Professor Neustadt and others have produced a number of other case studies about the swine flu incident as well.

[12] Gavetti, G., and Jan Rivkin. (2005). "How Strategists Really Think: Tapping the Power of Analogy." *Harvard Business Review.* April: 54–63. Gavetti and Rivkin had published a stream of work on how firms use analogies to formulate competitive strategy. For instance, see the following articles: Gavetti, G., D. Levinthal, and J. Rivkin. (2005). "Strategy-Making in Novel and Complex Worlds: The Power of Analogy." *Strategic Management Journal.* 26(8): 691–712; Gavetti, G. and J. Rivkin. (2004). "Teaching Students How to Reason Well by Analogy." *Journal of Strategic Management Education.* 1(2).

[13] Abelson, J. "High-concept cleaners in tatters." *Boston Globe.* May 15, 2008.

[14] For an interesting history of how Staples was created, see Stemberg, T. (1996). *Staples for Success: From Business Plan to Billion-Dollar Business in Just a Decade.* Santa Monica, CA: Knowledge Exchange.

[15] Interview with T. Krasnow, founder and former chief executive officer of Zoots. Krasnow and I worked at Staples together at the same time, although I was only a project manager working on acquisition integration efforts while Krasnow served as executive vice president of marketing. When I was teaching at the Harvard Business School, Krasnow was kind enough to come back and speak with some of my students about his professional experiences at Staples and Zoots. He also granted me an interview to talk about Zoots soon after he stepped down as chief executive officer.

[16] Abelson, J. (2008).

[17] Carroll, G. and G. Powell. (2003). "Cocoa Pete's Chocolate Adventures." Stanford Business School Case Study No. E153.

[18] Ibid.

[19] For a superb scholarly examination of the Enron collapse, see Salter, M. (2008). *Innovation Corrupted: The Origins and Legacy of Enron's Collapse.* Cambridge, MA: Harvard University Press. Mal Salter also has produced a case study that instructors might want to use when teaching about the Enron collapse. See Salter, M. (2003). "Innovation corrupted: The rise and fall of Enron (A) and (B)." Harvard Business School Case Study No. 904-036.

[20] This section is based on interviews I conducted at Enron with David Carvin, Joseph Bower, and Lynne Levesque of Harvard Business School in 2001 before the firm entered bankruptcy.

[21] Neustadt, R. and E. May. (1986). p. 39.

[22] Ibid.

[23] Neustadt, R. and E. May. (1986). p. 36. See also Truman, H. (1955–1956). *Memoirs.* Volume II. New York: Doubleday. pp. 332–333.

[24] Neustadt, R. and E. May. (1986). p. 43.

[25] Neustadt, R. and E. May. (1986). p. 44.

[26] For more on Truman's decision-making with regard to the Korean War, see McCullough, D. (1992). *Truman.* New York: Simon and Schuster. I also learned a great deal about President Truman's leadership and decision-making style when David McCullough came to Bryant University to deliver a speech about the American presidency on April 24, 2008.

[27] For more on active listening, with a particular emphasis on health care applications, see Robertson, K. (2005). "Active listening: More than just paying attention." *Australian Family Physician.* 34(12):1053–1055. In addition, see the following articles: Phelan, T. (1994). *1-2-3 Magic: Effective Discipline for Children 2–12.* Glen Ellyn, Illinois: Child Management Inc.; Korsgaard, M., D. Schweiger, and H. Sapienza. (1995). "Building commitment, attachment, and trust in strategic decision-making teams: The role of procedural justice." *Academy of Management Journal.* 38(1): p. 60–84.

[28] For an article on how to deal with blame effectively, see Baldwin, D. (2001). "How to win the blame game." *Harvard Business Review.* July/August: 55–60.

[29] Interview with Mario Shiliashki, Director of Finance, PayPal. Note that PayPal is a subsidiary of eBay, where I learned about another interesting story of pattern recognition. Nearly a decade ago, I had the opportunity to have breakfast with eBay CEO Meg Whitman, along with a few of my faculty colleagues. Whitman recounted an interesting story of pattern recognition to me at that time. She described how the firm tried to identify patterns in the buying and selling of goods on the site. She told us of a young manager who had noticed that a small market for used cars seemed to be emerging on the auction site in 1999. That manager also recognized the constraints that limited the potential of this market. For instance, most buyers wanted some sort of third-party endorsement of the quality and safety of the vehicle. Thus, the manager arranged inspection services to help reassure prospective buyers. This service and others like it helped create a much more viable market, and eBay's automobile sales took off. As it turns out, this manager was Simon Rothman, a classmate of mine from Harvard Business School who sat next to me for the second half of my first year in the MBA program!

[30] These thoughts on the case method benefit greatly from my conversations with many students over the years at Bryant University, New York University's Stern School of Business, and Harvard Business School.

[31] Former Secretary of Defense Robert McNamara shared these thoughts with me when he visited my class at the Harvard Business School in the spring of 2005.

5

Connect the Dots

"Creativity is the power to connect the seemingly unconnected."
—William Plomer, South African novelist

In the wake of the tragic events of September 11, 2001, various inquiries examined whether the U.S. intelligence community had failed to detect signs that a massive terrorist attack would take place. These inquiries determined that assorted bits of information had emerged in the months prior to 9/11, pointing to the possibility of a terrorist attack on American soil. Disparate pieces of information surfaced in parts of the intelligence community, including the Central Intelligence Agency (CIA), Federal Bureau of Investigation (FBI), and National Security Agency (NSA). However, people did not share key information swiftly and efficiently both within and across these organizations. No single entity or individual ever had access to all the data that suggested a possible attack. In a U.S. Congress report on intelligence failures prior to 9/11, Senator Richard Shelby concluded:

> "Our Joint Inquiry has highlighted fundamental problems with information-sharing within the Intelligence Community, depriving analysts of the information access they need in order to draw inferences and develop the conclusions necessary to inform decision-making. The Intelligence Community's abject failure to 'connect the dots' before September 11, 2001 illustrates the need to wholly re-think the Community's approach to these issues."[1]

In this chapter, we will examine why sufficient information sharing does not take place in many groups and organizations. Moreover, we will describe how leaders can facilitate more effective information sharing so that people can "connect the dots" among bits of data that, when synthesized and integrated, signal a potentially significant problem for the firm. Let's begin by taking a closer look at the intelligence community's actions prior to the 9/11 terrorist attacks. What signals existed, and why did the intelligence community fail to "connect the dots"?

"The System Was Blinking Red"

In the months leading up to the 9/11 terrorist attacks, a steady drumbeat of "frequent but fragmentary" reports began to emerge, pointing to the possibility of a terrorist attack.[2] The information came in bits and pieces, and it often proved rather ambiguous. Intelligence officials noted the increased level of al Qaeda propaganda, recruiting, and "chatter" during this time period. Various agencies received tips about possible attacks against American interests, both domestic and abroad, but the information often tended to be quite vague. The CIA did not have specific, credible information about the nature and location of possible attacks. Still, CIA Director George Tenet noted that "the system was blinking red" during the summer months.[3] As it turns out, much more specific information about the 9/11 attacks did exist that no one managed to synthesize and integrate in the summer of 2001. In particular, three separate investigations produced information that was not shared broadly, thereby making it impossible for any senior intelligence official to "connect the dots" prior to 9/11. The information stemmed from a CIA investigation of a terrorist meeting in Kuala Lumpur, as well as from investigations taking place in the Phoenix and Minneapolis field offices of the FBI in the summer of 2001. We cannot say for certain that the attacks would have been thwarted if all this information had been shared, but the probability of disrupting the plot certainly would have risen with more effective intelligence sharing and synthesis.

The CIA in Kuala Lumpur

In the late 1990s, a man named Khalid Sheikh Mohammed persuaded al Qaeda leader Usama Bin Ladin to go ahead with a plan to crash airplanes into U.S. buildings. Soon thereafter, Bin Ladin recruited two Saudis—Khalid al Mihdhar and Nawaf al Hazmi—to work on this plan. The two men attended al Qaeda training at Afghan camps and then traveled to Kuala Lumpur for a key meeting about the "planes operation." The National Security Agency (NSA) learned about the terrorist meeting set to take place, and CIA agents tracked Mihdhar to Kuala Lumpur. The agents observed the meeting, after which the terrorists fled to Thailand. At this time, the CIA knew that Mihdhar possessed a multiple-entry visa allowing him to come to the United States. The CIA did not add their names to the TIPOFF terrorist watch list maintained by the State Department, and it did not tell the FBI that these two individuals had visas permitting entry into the United States. The CIA learned that Hazmi traveled from Thailand to the United States in January 2000. The agency did not inform other units of the federal government about his arrival.

No federal agency tracked Mihdhar and Hazmi when they arrived in California in January 2000. The two men used their real names to open bank accounts, obtain driver's licenses, and attend flight schools. Mihdhar actually left the country in June 2000. While he was overseas, the CIA linked him to the attack on the USS *Cole*. However, the agency did not inform the State Department, which issued Mihdhar a new visa permitting him to return to the United States in July 2001.

During the summer of 2001, the CIA's Bin Ladin unit dug deeper into the connection of these two men to the USS *Cole* bombing. On

August 21, 2001, the CIA contacted the Immigration and Naturaliza-
tion Service (the INS was then located within the State Department)
about Mihdhar and Hazmi. The INS reported that the two men had
already arrived in the United States.

In late August, an FBI analyst assigned to work in the CIA's Bin
Ladin unit sent a memo about the two men to the FBI's New York
Field Office. The memo requested that agents begin to search for
Mihdhar and Hazmi. No one communicated this information to FBI
headquarters. Confusion regarding FBI rules about the handling of
intelligence investigations hampered the search. The New York agent
assigned to the matter began trying to find the two men, but he did
not make substantial progress in the few remaining days prior to
September 11.

The Phoenix Memo

On July 10, 2001, an FBI agent in Phoenix, Arizona sent a
memo to FBI headquarters, as well as to the New York Field
Office. His memo stated:

> "The purpose of this communication is to advise the Bureau
> and New York of the possibility of a coordinated effort by
> Usama Bin Ladin to send students to the United States to
> attend civil aviation universities and colleges. Phoenix has
> observed an inordinate number of individuals of investigative
> interest who are attending or who have attended civil aviation
> universities and colleges in the State of Arizona... These indi-
> viduals will be in a position in the future to conduct terror
> activity against civil aviation targets."[4]

One year earlier, Phoenix agent Kenneth Williams had learned
that Zackaria Soubra had enrolled in aviation courses at a local university. Soubra had organized a number of anti-U.S. and anti-Israeli
rallies in which he called for jihad. An organization to which he
belonged had issued several statements suggesting airports as potential targets. Williams' investigation further revealed that Soubra had a

connection to a man who tried to gain access to the cockpit of a commercial airliner in 1999. The FBI actually had interrogated Soubra's associate, but the Bureau released him when the man stated that he believed the door led to the bathroom, not the cockpit.

Williams interviewed Soubra several times in the spring of 2000, and Williams became concerned when he saw a poster of Bin Ladin in Soubra's home. Soubra admitted to Williams that he believed United States government entities were "legitimate military targets of Islam."[5] Soubra also informed the agent that he endorsed prior al Qaeda attacks against overseas interests of the United States.

Williams later discovered that other Sunni Muslims with connections to Soubra, and holding similar radical views, had enrolled at a flight school in Arizona. His investigation identified six individuals obtaining flight training and one studying aviation security. With this information, Williams crafted his July 2001 memo to FBI headquarters. The agent made four recommendations. He wanted to compile a list of civil aviation schools in the United States, make contact with those schools, obtain visa information for students in those institutions, and discuss his investigation more broadly with other officials in the intelligence community. The agents in the Bin Ladin unit examined the memo, but they did not share it with their bosses, other units within the Bureau, or senior executives. They did not act on his recommendations. The headquarters agents also did not share the memo with other government agencies, such as the CIA.[6]

The Minneapolis Field Office Investigation

In August 2001, FBI agents in the Minneapolis Field Office learned that a man named Zacarias Moussaoui had enrolled at Pan Am International Flight Academy in Eagan, Minnesota. He stood out there for several reasons. First, he wanted the instructors to teach him how to "take off and land" a Boeing 747 aircraft, even though he did not work for a commercial airline, nor did he intend to seek employment at one of those firms.[7] He did not even have a pilot's license of any kind. Moussaoui also paid cash for the training—the rather hefty sum of $6,800.

FBI agents discovered that Moussaoui believed in the notion of waging jihad against the United States. When questioned about his religious beliefs, Moussaoui tended to become perturbed. Based on his past travels, agents believed that Moussaoui may have traveled to al Qaeda training camps in Afghanistan. When they questioned him about the camps, he became agitated. Minneapolis agents began to suspect that Moussaoui "was an Islamic extremist preparing for some future act in furtherance of radical fundamentalist goals."[8] They worried that he wanted to learn to fly Boeing 747 airplanes because he was planning a major hijacking.

The INS detained Moussaoui on August 17 because he had overstayed his visa. The Minneapolis agents wanted a special warrant to search Moussaoui's computer and other belongings. A conflict arose between the field office and headquarters regarding whether sufficient evidence existed for a special Foreign Intelligence and Surveillance Act (FISA) warrant. A contentious phone call between headquarters and the field office took place in the final days of August. A headquarters official remarked that the Minneapolis agents were overreacting to the Moussaoui situation. Remarkably, a field office supervisor replied that he was simply trying to ensure that Moussaoui "did not take control of a plane and fly it into the World Trade Center."[9] The headquarters agent replied, "That's not going to happen. We don't know he's a terrorist. You don't have enough to show he is a terrorist. You have a guy interested in this type of aircraft—that is it."[10] No one briefed senior FBI officials about the Minneapolis investigation prior to the 9/11 attacks.

The 9/11 Attacks

On September 11, 2001, Mihdhar and Hazmi served as "muscle hijackers" on American Airlines Flight 77, which crashed into the

Pentagon. They had come into and out of the United States with relative ease over the past two years, despite CIA knowledge of their terrorist activities and concerns about their ties to the USS *Cole* bombing. The State Department and FBI did not track these individuals due to the lack of information sharing by the CIA. The individuals identified in the Phoenix memo did not take part in the hijackings. However, at least one student investigated by Kenneth Williams had ties to a 9/11 hijacker. Moussaoui remained in custody on September 11 due to his visa violation, while the FBI had not pursued its investigation due to the lack of a FISA warrant. As it turns out, the FBI later learned that Moussaoui had ties to the terrorists onboard the planes that were hijacked. He eventually pled guilty to conspiring with al Qaeda to attack the United States.

Williams had no knowledge that Minneapolis agents had been conducting an investigation into flight training performed by a radical fundamentalist. Likewise, the Minneapolis field office did not know about the Phoenix investigation. The headquarters agents who denied the Minneapolis field office's warrant request had no knowledge of the Phoenix memo prior to the attacks. The CIA, which had learned of the Moussaoui investigation prior to 9/11, also had no knowledge of the investigation in Arizona. Williams noted, "It's been my past experience that the smallest bit of information that comes in could later turn out to be the most important piece of the investigation."[11] Coleen Rowley, Chief Division Counsel of the Minneapolis Field Office, testified to Congress, "The need for people at FBI Headquarters who can connect the dots is painfully obvious."[12] The Joint Inquiry by the U.S. Senate and House Intelligence Committees faulted all the agencies of the intelligence community for a lack of adequate information sharing. It concluded that better dissemination of intelligence might have enabled someone to connect these three investigative threads to one another, as well as to the broader increase in threat reporting that took place in the summer of 2001.

Why Not Share Information?

In the case of the U.S. intelligence community, many reasons exist for the inadequate information sharing prior to the 9/11 attacks. Some of those reasons prove to be quite specific to intelligence issues. For instance, officials often guard intelligence data closely because they do not want to compromise its security. They worry about leaks, as well as accidental disclosure of the information. Moreover, officials worry that their sources might be compromised. The rules for securing special warrants on intelligence investigations also hindered information sharing prior to 9/11. While these issues certainly are peculiar to the intelligence community, the 9/11 case also highlights many broader obstacles that impede information sharing in a range of organizations, in both the private and public sectors.

All complex organizations must balance the need for differentiation with the need for integration, as scholars Paul Lawrence and Jay Lorsch have explained.[13] Differentiation refers to how firms get work done by creating specialized units that become experts at focusing on particular dimensions of the organization's mission. In a business, corporations might create specialized units that focus on particular products, customers, and/or geographies. Lawrence and Lorsch argue that the most successful firms balance that specialization with integration— alignment and coordination among the firm's differentiated units.

Striking the right balance can be quite difficult, though, particularly as organizations grow in size and complexity. Specialized units of an organization often develop their own identity, but people sometimes develop a closer affiliation to their unit than to the organization as a whole. They might go so far as to disparage the culture and identity of other units. Moreover, specialized departments hold divergent interests at times. Conflicting goals and objectives among differentiated units inevitably lead to "thick walls" among the "silos" inside some organizations. No organization with sufficient levels of differentiation can ever create subunits whose goals are completely aligned.

Many organizations benefit from healthy competition among differentiated units, and they purposefully induce such rivalry. Witness the many businesses that rank divisions against one another, handsomely rewarding those units that outperform their peers. At times, however, such competition can become destructive, with one unit benefiting at another's expense, while collaborative opportunities fall by the wayside.

For the intelligence community prior to 9/11, federal officials tended to place a premium on the need for differentiation, with less focus on integration (as my colleague Jan Rivkin pointed out when we conducted this research together).[14] They did so because they wanted multiple sources and perspectives on intelligence. Officials believed that some level of competition among disparate parts of the intelligence community would protect against errors arising from "groupthink" behavior within any particular agency. Moreover, each agency had its own goals and objectives, beyond protecting against terrorist threats. The FBI, for instance, maintained a primary mission of fighting crime; intelligence collection proved secondary prior to 9/11. The Defense Department focused on military preparedness, the CIA on intelligence regarding foreign nation-states, and so on.

Many organizations face a similar dilemma, where the need for a high level of differentiation leads to substantial barriers that prevent adequate integration. For many firms, the lack of integration does not prove costly until a substantial shift occurs in the external environment. That turbulence, and the new threats it creates, often require much more information sharing and coordination among differentiated units. A similar problem occurred with regard to the intelligence community and the 9/11 attacks. The high level of differentiation served the country well, for the most part, during the Cold War. However, the new threat posed by the amorphous al Qaeda organization created a need for much more integration.

Concerns about power also impede information sharing within organizations. Everyone has heard the famous phrase "Knowledge is power"—a statement often attributed to Sir Francis Bacon.

Organizational subunits do hoard information at times because they recognize that access to critical data brings with it a certain amount of leverage and perhaps glory too. In the case of the intelligence community, Senator Shelby notes that "knowledge *literally* is power...the bureaucratic importance of an agency depends upon supposedly 'unique' contributions to national security it can make by monopolizing control of 'its' data stream."[15] The same power dynamics come into play in business enterprises. For instance, managers may not want to provide others with access to a key customer because they want the credit for the revenues generated by that client, and because they want to maximize their personal importance in the eyes of senior executives.

Information Sharing in Small Groups

To this point, we have focused on the information-sharing problems that make it difficult for leaders to "connect the dots" in large, complex organizations. However, information-sharing troubles are not the exclusive provenance of big bureaucracies. Research shows that even small teams face substantial hurdles when it comes to the dissemination and synthesis of information possessed by various members.

In 1985, Garold Stasser and William Titus conducted a study that "challenged the idea that group decisions are more informed than individual decisions."[16] They created four-person groups and asked them to make a decision. Stasser and Titus compared the team decision quality with the choices made by individuals given the same information. When all team members possessed the same information, the group decision exceeded the quality of individual choices. However, the scholars then created a scenario in which each member possessed unique information that his or her colleagues did not have. To arrive at the optimal decision, individuals needed to share their privately held information. The results showed that "groups were more likely to endorse an inferior option after discussion than were their individual members before discussion."[17] The scholars surmised that the groups must have had difficulties surfacing all privately held information.[18]

A subsequent study by Stasser and colleagues further explored the information-sharing difficulties encountered by small groups. In this research project, the scholars recorded the team discussions. Each individual had information common to all of his or her colleagues, as well as pieces of privately held information not provided to other team members. The scholars discovered the following:

> "Effective information pooling is not simply a matter of promoting the discussion of unique information. It also requires that decision making groups use unique information to inform their decisions... About a third of the common items were repeated at least once after they were first discussed but only a fourth of unique items were repeated. The message was clear. Not only were unique items less likely to be mentioned during discussion, but they were also more likely to be ignored once they were mentioned."[19]

Other scholars have confirmed Stasser's findings.[20] In groups where information is distributed unequally among the members, *people tend to surface and discuss commonly held information much more so than privately held information.* The failure to adequately share, discuss, and analyze uniquely held information inhibits the effectiveness of group problem-solving. One should remember that this information-sharing problem exists in small groups, even in these experimental settings where the team members' interests are completely aligned, and where power concerns do not seem to be substantial. Amy Edmondson, Michael Watkins, and I have argued that these breakdowns in team decision-making only get worse—perhaps far worse—when group members maintain partially divergent goals and objectives, as is often the case with management teams in organizations.[21] In sum, the intelligence community's failure to "connect the dots" should not simply be attributed to the size and complexity of the bureaucracy. The research shows that many teams, as small as four members, have trouble sharing and integrating information.

Why do members of small groups fail to share information, even when their interests are aligned? Psychologists do not know for certain, but Stasser has argued that perhaps "the bearer of unique information, like the bearer of bad news, incurs some social costs... these social costs may include the necessity of establishing the credibility and relevance of the unique information."[22] Stasser also points out that status dynamics may exacerbate the problem. In a study by James Larson and colleagues, medical residents, interns, and third-year medical school students examined information relating to a patient's symptoms. They found that residents were substantially more likely to repeat unique information than interns or students. They also asked more questions about unique information that came to light. This finding suggests that lower-status members of a group may feel a particularly heavy burden associated with the social costs of surfacing private information.[23] In sum, "connecting the dots" should not be viewed as a problem solely of the large, complex organization; it plagues small groups as well due to fundamental psychological processes and interpersonal dynamics common to many workplace teams.

How to Facilitate Information Sharing

How can leaders overcome information-sharing barriers so that they can "connect the dots" more effectively? How can they surface and synthesize disparate bits of data so as to identify significant problems and threats in their organizations? Let's begin by focusing on how leaders can "connect the dots" more effectively within the small teams they manage. Then we will turn to the challenge of information sharing and integration across units of a large organization.

Leading Teams

One might think that a consensus-oriented, participative leadership style will encourage more communication and information sharing within your team, while a directive approach hinders information flow. However, the research evidence provides an interesting twist on this conventional wisdom. James Larson and his colleagues contrasted participative and directive leaders. They defined the former as leaders who shared power with their subordinates and who withheld their views until others had been given an opportunity to voice their opinions. These scholars defined directive leaders as those who took charge and stated their views at the outset, while often playing devil's advocate as other opinions surfaced. Larson and his colleagues discovered that participative leaders tend to surface more privately held information. However, more directive leaders tended to repeat unshared information more often, even when that data did not support their viewpoint. Therefore, a directive leadership approach may encourage a group to analyze unshared data more closely and actually incorporate it into the team's decision-making process.[24]

Directive leaders have to be careful, though, because a forceful statement of their views at the outset might quash dissenting views and hinder candid dialogue. Deference to the boss can become quite problematic if leaders become overly directive. Amy Edmondson, Michael Watkins, and I have argued that leaders can avoid that problem by *adopting a directive approach to facilitating the group process, while not trying to dictate the content of the decision.* Rather than stating their views at the outset, leaders might consider focusing on their facilitation skills. They might intervene actively to surface privately held information, drawing people into a lively and vigorous dialogue. Moreover, they can highlight key pieces of private information and ensure that the team pays adequate attention to this data. These *process interventions* can help a team "connect the dots" while not suppressing the level of constructive debate.[25]

What types of behaviors can leaders engage in to encourage more effective handling of information? First, they can "manage airtime," ensuring that a few people do not dominate the discussion. Leaders should actively seek out the quiet members of the group and encourage them to participate. Second, leaders ought to reiterate and/or paraphrase ideas and statements that emerged quickly but perhaps did not receive adequate attention from most members of the team. By playing back what they have heard, leaders can test their interpretation of the new data, and also ensure that others catch ideas they may have missed at first. Third, leaders should ask clarifying questions as people bring forward new information. They also can question other team members to ensure that they have understood the new points that have been raised. Such inquiries not only clarify understanding, but also flush out additional data that may not have yet surfaced. Finally, leaders should encourage people to express alternative viewpoints and, at times, induce debates so as to surface more data and assumptions.

Perhaps most importantly, leaders need to take time near the end of a decision-making process to highlight the areas of remaining uncertainty that would ideally be resolved before making a decision. In so doing, leaders can ask the following types of questions:

- What else would we like to know in order to make a good decision?
- Have we made some assumptions that could be validated through additional information gathering?
- Would additional data resolve the differences of opinion within the group?
- Where could we find that information?
- Does anyone have access to that type of data?

By asking these kinds of questions, leaders can stress the gaps in the team's knowledge base and stimulate a search to close those gaps. In so doing, leaders can draw out information that still has not surfaced. Throughout this lively dialogue, leaders must explicitly ask the team to consider the links among various bits of information. They should probe for connections as well as for inconsistencies. They must encourage a process of synthesis and integration, not simply a contentious give-and-take among alternative viewpoints.[26]

Leading Organizations

In large, complex organizations, many leaders may adopt structural solutions to information-sharing problems. Often, the new structures focus on the vertical flow of information, and they involve increased centralization and an additional level to the organizational hierarchy. Consider the structural reforms made in the intelligence community after the 9/11 attacks. Government officials decided to create two new entities to facilitate the sharing and integration of intelligence: the Department of Homeland Security (DHS) and the Office of the Director of National Intelligence (DNI).

Both new structures involved a substantial increase in centralization, as well as an additional level in the organizational hierarchy. Clearly, some benefits may emerge. The DNI, for instance, may be able to examine and synthesize various bits of intelligence collected and analyzed by the CIA, FBI, and others. Perhaps they can "connect the dots" effectively among disparate pieces of information. However, serious risks emerge with this type of structure. The additional hierarchy and structural complexity can make it even more difficult for "bad news" or dissenting views to rise to the top of the government bureaucracy. Moreover, the DNI may limit the range of perspectives presented to top officials. In synthesizing what they have heard from various intelligence agencies, the DNI may be tempted to speak with "one voice" to the president and other senior officials. It may be more effective, however, if top decision-makers hear competing and divergent stories from various intelligence agencies. In sum, no structural change provides a perfect solution to the information-sharing problem. All structural reforms have costs and benefits.

Leaders do have an alternative to simple and sometimes problematic structural solutions that focus primarily on the vertical flow of information. They can and should foster the expansion and utilization of informal social networks. As Tiziano Casciaro and Miguel Sousa Lobo wrote in a recent *Harvard Business Review* article:

> "How do you ensure that relevant information gets transferred between two parts of an organization that have different cultures... The answers to such questions lie not in an examination of organization charts but largely in an understanding of informal social networks and how they emerge. Certainly, organizations are designed to ensure that people interact in ways necessary to get their jobs done. But all kinds of work-related encounters and relationships exist that only partly reflect these purposefully designed structures. Even in the context of formal structures like cross-functional teams, informal relationships play a major role."[27]

Leaders can foster the formation and development of social networks through activities such as job rotation programs, the creation of informal gathering places, off-site retreats, and leadership development programs. For instance, job rotations expose people to other units in the organization. Those rotations help foster better understanding and appreciation of the work being done in other units. They also help individuals build their social networks. Then, people know precisely who they should ask for critical information in the future.

Sociologist Ronald Burt has argued that we should focus our attention on the precise structure of social networks if we hope to foster more effective information sharing. In most organizations, clusters of people exist within which individuals tend to speak with one another and exchange information quite frequently. However, a cluster may not have strong ties to other groups within the organization. Burt described the paucity of connections between any two groups as "structural holes" in the social network of the organization. He argued that a few individuals may span the holes though. In short, several people within a particular group may possess strong ties to other individuals in an otherwise disconnected cluster. Therefore, they have the ability to serve as "brokers" who facilitate the flow of information across the structural holes. To help connect the dots more effectively, we need to identify and leverage these critical brokers within the social networks of our organizations.[28]

Beyond social networks, leaders also can use technology and mass-collaboration techniques to marshal the collective knowledge and intellect of many people throughout an organization. In so doing, they can take advantage of the "wisdom of crowds." In his best-selling book by that name, James Surowiecki argues that we can get effective solutions to many problems by pooling the conclusions and insights of many people without even asking them to communicate and interact with one another. He gives the simple example of the game show *Who Wants to Be a Millionaire?*. As you may know, contestants have several techniques they can employ to help them answer a difficult question. For instance, they can "ask the audience," in which case the audience votes on which of the four possible answers is correct. Surowiecki points out that the random group of people in the audience selects the correct answer 91% of the time. He provides many examples such as this one, and he argues that the aggregation of information in this manner provides better-quality decisions than most individual experts can make.[29]

Many companies have taken advantage of mass collaboration and the wisdom of crowds. For instance, in their book titled *Wikinomics: How Mass Collaboration Changes Everything*, Dan Tapscott and Anthony Williams describe how a Toronto mining company created a contest. People around the world could examine the company's geological data and offer a recommendation as to where to search for gold on its properties. The contest yielded solutions that had eluded the company's in-house experts.[30]

The intelligence community has adopted "wiki" technology and mass-collaboration techniques as well. *Wall Street Journal* columnist Gordon Crovitz explains:

"The federal government has launched several wikis, which permit staffers to post information and expand on it until a consensus has been reached. Intellipedia lets 37,000 officials at the CIA, FBI, NSA, and other U.S. intelligence agencies share information and even rate one another for accuracy in password-protected wikis, some 'top secret.' Users are told, 'We want your knowledge, not your agency seal'; indeed, the wiki format may be the best last hope for connecting the dots of intelligence across sixteen different agencies."[31]

Mindset Matters

After 9/11, FBI Director Robert Mueller and his top team had to reshape the Bureau.[32] Above all else, they had to change the mindset and the culture within the organization. Throughout its history, the Bureau focused primarily on investigating crimes after they occurred. Now, it had to focus on gathering intelligence proactively so as to prevent crimes before they happened. Detecting potential problems, with little public attention or praise, had to become as highly valued and rewarded as heroically solving crimes and arresting perpetrators. Senior counterterrorism official Arthur Cummings explained the shift toward a "prevent first" mindset that would have to occur:

"The agent's job now isn't just to arrest bad guys. It is to understand everything in the terrorist's head, everything around him, so that we can understand his world and the world of those around him... After 9/11, we have to subordinate the desire to arrest and prosecute quickly because often there is more value to waiting, watching, and collecting more intelligence. If the threat is imminent, we might have to make an arrest so as to disrupt the terrorist plot. But, in many cases, it is more productive to wait. Before 9/11, we were a law enforcement agency with the power to gather domestic intelligence. Now, we have to become a domestic intelligence service with law enforcement powers."[33]

Many observers expressed skepticism as to whether the Bureau could accomplish this shift in mindset. As one long-time investigator for a Senate committee responsible for FBI oversight put it, "Mueller is essentially waging two wars at the same time: one against terrorism and one against his own bureaucracy. They are not geared up for prevention of anything. They are geared up to arrest someone after a crime has been committed."[34] In fact, the traditional metrics for measuring agent performance focused on the number of arrests and prosecutions. Agents achieved promotions by solving crimes and "putting bad guys behind bars." Waiting and watching for months, without making arrests, simply did not fit the "can-do" attitude of most agents. The cultural shift proved to be quite substantial, and it has taken years for the Bureau to shift toward a problem-finding mindset, where people feel equally satisfied and rewarded for detecting potential threats as compared to solving crimes that have already occurred. Mueller has made progress, but much work remains to be done.

All leaders who want to become better problem-finders have to accomplish this shift in mindset. They have to make detecting problems a priority, rather than simply making heroes of those who put out the fires in the organization. They must recognize that those who discover and prevent problems often do not get rewarded, nor are they heralded by their peers. The problem-solvers tend to get the most attention. People often do not even know about the problems that have been prevented.

To become more effective at "connecting the dots," leaders need to embrace one other mindset change. It involves how we think through problems and situations. According to Roger Martin, Dean of the Rotman School of Management, the most effective leaders nurture and develop their integrative thinking skills.[35] By that, he means that they hone their ability to synthesize opposing ideas and discordant information. Martin identifies four ways in which the best integrative thinkers distinguish themselves from conventional ones. First, integrative thinkers search extensively and proactively for "less obvious but potentially relevant factors" in a situation.[36] They "don't mind a messy problem. In fact, they welcome complexity, because that's where the best answers come from."[37] Second, they do not assume simple linear cause-and-effect relationships. They recognize that most outcomes have multiple causes. Third, integrative thinkers "see problems as a whole."[38] They examine situations and organizations from a systemic perspective rather than looking separately at each part. They understand that parts of a system interact in unpredictable ways, and that one element in a system can magnify the effect of a change in other areas. Finally, integrative thinkers do not simply make either-or choices. They try to generate innovative ideas by combining and synthesizing many pieces of information as well as different and perhaps conflicting ideas.

Martin believes that we can nurture our integrative thinking skills; they are not simply a product of our genes. He's right. To become more effective at "connecting the dots," leaders must attract, retain, and develop the integrative thinkers in their organizations, while attending to their own integrative skills. We must learn to see problems as a whole, recognizing that most complex failures (or successes) do not have a single cause. We have to recognize that leaders need to do more than surface crucial information; synthesis indeed represents one of the most important responsibilities of a leader.

Endnotes

[1] Shelby, R. (2002). "September 11 and the imperative reform in the U.S. intelligence community: Additional views of Senator Richard Shelby, Vice chairman, Senate Select Committee on Intelligence." pp. 4–5. Malcolm Gladwell has written an interesting essay in response to Shelby's conclusions. See Gladwell, M. "Connecting the dots: The paradoxes of intelligence reform." *The New Yorker*. March 10, 2003.

[2] This section draws heavily on the case study, cited in Chapter 1, about the 9/11 terrorist attacks; see Rivkin, J., M. Roberto, and E. Ferlins. (2006). "Managing National Intelligence (A): Before 9/11." Harvard Business School Case Study No. 9-706-463. That case study, in turn, draws heavily upon the 9/11 Commission's work: *The 9/11 Commission Report: Final Report of the National Commission on Terrorist Attacks Upon the United States*. (2004). New York: W.W. Norton & Company.

[3] *The 9/11 Commission Report: Final Report of the National Commission on Terrorist Attacks Upon the United States.* (2004). New York: W.W. Norton & Company. p. 254.

[4] http://www.thememoryhole.org/911/phoenix-memo/.

[5] Ibid.

[6] *The 9/11 Commission Report: Final Report of the National Commission on Terrorist Attacks Upon the United States.* (2004). New York: W.W. Norton & Company, p. 272.

[7] Ibid, p. 273.

[8] Ibid.

[9] Ibid, p. 275.

[10] Ibid.

[11] Poniewozik, J. "The man behind the memo." *Time.* November 26, 2001.

[12] Colleen Rowley, Testimony to the United States Senate Committee on the Judiciary, Oversight Hearing on Counterterrorism, June 6, 2002.

[13] Lawrence, P. and J. Lorsch. (1967). *Organization and Environment: Managing Differentiation and Integration.* Boston: Harvard Business School Division of Research.

[14] Jan Rivkin drew these connections as we discussed how to teach our case study on the 9/11 attacks. We both owe a debt of gratitude to Jay Lorsch, who we have had the privilege of learning from over the years. Lawrence and Lorsch's contingency theory continues to stand out as one of the seminal events in the history of the evolution of organizational theory. In my view, every doctoral student in management ought to read their 1967 book during their first semester in graduate school. In my case, I had the privilege of taking a course with Jay Lorsch in graduate school, in which he took us through many of the classic readings in organizational theory, stretching all the way back to the works of Frederick Taylor, Mary Parker Follett, Chester Barnard, and others of their time.

[15] Shelby, R. (2002). p. 22.

[16] Stasser, G. and W. Titus. (2003). "Hidden profiles: A brief history." *Psychological Inquiry.* 14(3/4): 304–313. The quotation is from page 304 of that article. The original research was published in 1985. Stasser, G. and W. Titus. (1985). "Pooling of unshared information in group decision making: Biased information sampling during discussion." *Journal of Personality and Social Psychology.* (48): 1467–1478.

[17] Stasser, G. and W. Titus. (2003). p. 305.

[18] Many people hail the promise of teamwork and collaboration in organizations. When individuals pool their knowledge and expertise, presumably a synergy may occur, in which the whole proves greater than the sum of the parts. Unfortunately, research shows that many teams do not achieve this expected synergy. Team researchers use the term "process losses" to describe how a group's actual performance may fall short of its potential performance. See Steiner, I. D. (1972). *Group*

Process and Productivity. New York: Academic Press. The inability to share and integrate privately held information constitutes one important type of group process loss.

[19] Stasser, G. and W. Titus. (2003). p. 308. The study in which the conversations were recorded was published in 1989. Stasser, G., L. Taylor, and C. Hanna. (1989). "Information sampling in structured and unstructured discussions of three and six-person groups." *Journal of Personality and Social Psychology*. 57: 67–78.

[20] For example, see Larson, J., C. Christensen, A. Abbott, and T. Franz. (1996). "Diagnosing groups: Charting the flow of information in medical decision making teams." *Journal of Personality and Social Psychology*. (71): 315–330.

[21] Edmondson, A., M. Roberto, and M. Watkins. (2003). "A Dynamic Model of Top Management Team Effectiveness: Managing Unstructured Task Streams." *Leadership Quarterly*. 14(3): 297–325.

[22] Stasser, G. and W. Titus. (2003). p. 308.

[23] Larson, J., C. Christensen, A. Abbott, and T. Franz. (1996).

[24] Larson, J., P. Foster-Fishman, and T. Franz. (1998). "Leadership style and the discussion of shared and unshared information in decision-making groups." *Personality and Social Psychology Bulletin*. 24(5): 482–495.

[25] Edmondson, A., M. Roberto, and M. Watkins. (2003). See also Nadler, D. A. (1996). "Managing the team at the top." *Strategy and Business*. 2: 42–51.

[26] For those who would like to teach these ideas around how to facilitate the sharing and discussion of shared and unshared information, Amy Edmondson and I have created a web-based leadership and team dynamics simulation. Roberto, M. and A. Edmondson. (2008). *Everest Leadership and Team Simulation*. Boston: Harvard Business School Publishing. We have published a comprehensive teaching note to help instructors run and then debrief this simulation. During the simulation, teams of students set out to "climb Mount Everest" and must solve a series of problems along the path to the summit. To solve the problems correctly, the team members must share private information with one another and integrate that information effectively.

[27] Casciaro, T. and M. Lobo. (2005). "Competent jerks, lovable fools and the formation of social networks." *Harvard Business Review*. June: 92–99.

[28] Burt, R. (1992). *Structural Holes: The Social Structure of Competition*. Cambridge, MA: Harvard University Press.

[29] Surowiecki, J. (2004). *The Wisdom of Crowds: Why the Many Are Smarter Than the Few and How Collective Wisdom Shapes Business, Economies, Societies and Nations*. New York: Anchor Books.

[30] Tapscott, D. and A. Williams. (2006). *Wikinomics: How Mass Collaboration Changes Everything*. New York: Penguin.

[31] Crovitz, G. "From Wikinomics to Government 2.0." *Wall Street Journal*. May 12, 2008. p. A13.

[32] This section draws on research that Jan Rivkin and I conducted at the Federal Bureau of Investigation in 2006–2007. We conducted interviews with many officials at the Bureau, stretching from FBI Director Robert Mueller to special agents working in field offices. Based on this research, we published two case studies about the FBI. The first takes the Bureau up through November 2001, with the case ending as Mueller ponders how to restructure the organization after the 9/11 attacks. The second case takes the student through the end of 2006; it charts many of the changes that Mueller enacted in the five years after the 9/11 attacks. The cases provide an unvarnished examination of the successes and failures that the FBI has experienced. We are very grateful to Director Mueller and his colleagues, particularly senior FBI national security branch executive Phil Mudd, for their willingness to be so candid with us about the challenges that the FBI faces in this transformation process. Rivkin, J. and M. Roberto. (2007). "Federal Bureau of Investigation (A)." Harvard Business School Case Study No. 9-707-500; Rivkin, J. and M. Roberto. (2007). "Federal Bureau of Investigation (B)." Harvard Business School Case Study No. 9-707-553.

[33] Rivkin, J. and M. Roberto. (2007). "Federal Bureau of Investigation (B)." Harvard Business School Case Study No. 9-707-553. p. 2.

[34] Eggen, D. and J. McGee. "FBI rushes to remake its mission." *Washington Post.* November 12, 2001. p. A1.

[35] Martin, R. (2007). "How successful leaders think." *Harvard Business Review.* June: 60–69.

[36] Ibid.

[37] Ibid.

[38] Ibid.

6

Encourage Useful Failures

"I have not failed. I've just found 10,000 ways that won't work."
—Thomas Edison

James Dyson hated the fact that vacuum cleaners often became clogged, lost suction, and left far too much dirt on the floor.[1] Described as a "tireless tinkerer," the British inventor began trying to solve these problems.[2] While Dyson tinkered, his wife's salary as an art teacher kept the family afloat. The couple grew their own vegetables, made their own clothes, and still, they sank deeper and deeper into debt. After many years, Dyson perfected his revolutionary bagless vacuum cleaner. The patented spinning technology separated dirt and dust from the air, eliminating the need for a filter or bag. The transparent design enabled the user to watch the cleaning process in action, something consumers enjoyed immensely.[3]

Dyson tried to persuade one of the multinational competitors in the market to manufacture the product. These companies resisted, because the product undermined their classic razor-and-blades business model. In other words, the incumbent firms sold vacuum cleaners at a modest margin and reaped huge rewards from an ongoing stream of replacement bag sales. Undeterred by their rejection, Dyson opened his own factory in the United Kingdom. The product became an international hit. Today, James Dyson ranks as one of the richest men in the world; *Forbes* estimates his net worth at $1.6 billion.[4] Queen Elizabeth II knighted him in December 2006. Despite all that success, Dyson loves talking about the importance of failure in his life as an industrial designer. "I made 5,127 prototypes of my vacuum before I got it right," said Dyson. "There were 5,126 failures, but I learned from each one. That's how I came up with a solution. So I don't mind failure."[5] He goes on to argue that we often fool ourselves into believing that successful products emerge from a moment of "effortless brilliance." To him, failures provide keen insights that enable the invention of unique products. Dyson explains:

> "We're taught to do things the right way. But if you want to discover something that other people haven't, you need to do things the wrong way. Initiate a failure by doing something that's very silly, unthinkable, naughty, dangerous. Watching why that fails can take you on a completely different path. It's exciting, actually."[6]

Alberto Alessi stresses the importance of failures too. Known as "the godfather of Italian design," Alessi joined his family's housewares company in 1970.[7] Over the past four decades, he and his brothers have transformed the firm into an avant-garde design house known for its partnerships with leading architects, designers, and artists such as Phillippe Starck, Michael Graves, and Ettore Sottsass. Alessi has created chic products, such as a lemon squeezer from Starck, a kettle from Graves, and oil and vinegar cruets by Sottsass.[8] Revenue has grown at a robust clip in recent years. Alessi readily acknowledges that the firm has made its share of mistakes, though. For instance, the Aldo Rossi Conical Kettle appeared aesthetically pleasing to consumers. Unfortunately, the handle becomes far too hot, rendering it unusable in most households. A phallic-shaped igniter for gas ranges turned out to be a bust too, while not surprisingly provoking a rebuke from Catholic Church leaders in Italy.[9] Alessi likes these fiascoes, believe it or not. He says, "I have to remind my brothers how vital it is to have one, possibly two, fiascoes per year. Should Alessi go for two or three years without a fiasco, we will be in danger of losing our leadership in design."[10]

At the company's headquarters, weekly design meetings take place in an interesting setting—the company's private museum, which prominently features Alessi's major flops. The company leaders want to remind the designers that no one has a perfect batting average, regardless of their creativity or effort. They want the designers not to be afraid to take risks, or to fear being punished for failures. Carlo Ricchetti, Alessi's head of production, explains, "We use the archive museum for designers who want to work with us to encourage them to experiment with new ideas and appreciate the value of good ideas."[11] Alessi expounds on this notion: "I like fiascoes, because they are the only moment when there is a flash of light that can help you see where the border between success and failure is."[12]

Many chief executives express a fervent desire to encourage risk-taking and innovation in their organizations. They proclaim that it's "OK to fail" at their firms. However, few leaders back up all that talk with action. The words from the top seem to ring hollow to many employees, who fear acknowledging their mistakes and failures. They believe that a misstep could cost them their job or, at a minimum, derail the upward trajectory of their careers. They recall far too many instances when their colleagues seemed to be punished for taking a risk and experiencing a failure.

Why Tolerate Failure?

Problem-finding requires a very different mindset with regard to failure. How does creating a culture that genuinely tolerates a healthy dose of risk-taking and failure help to surface the problems and threats facing a firm? First, if people fear punishment, they will be far less likely to admit mistakes and errors. Without an understanding of where and how these mistakes are occurring, senior leaders cannot spot patterns and trends. They cannot connect the dots among multiple incidents to identify major problems of and threats to the organization.

At Children's Hospital in Minneapolis, Chief Operating Officer Julie Morath instituted a "blameless reporting system" for medical accidents.[13] She empowered people to communicate confidentially and anonymously about medical accidents without being punished. Naturally, some errors, such as those involving negligence or malfeasance, were deemed "blameworthy acts." Most incidents, however, did not involve personal carelessness; they indicated more systemic problems at the hospital. Morath's initiative aimed to surface as many of the hospital's problems as possible so that she could identify the underlying causes of these accidents. She wanted to shine a light on errors to expose the vulnerabilities in the hospital's systems and processes. One physician commented about the aftermath of a procedure that did not go as planned: "It wasn't the old ABC model of medicine: Accuse, Blame, Criticize. What kicked in was a different model: blameless reporting. We sat down and filled out a safety report and acknowledged all the different components that went wrong and did root cause analyses."[14] The doctors and nurses implemented important system improvements as a result of those analyses. In fact, the number of medical errors reported by staff members actually rose after Morath instituted her blameless reporting system. The rise did not indicate more harm being done to patients, but rather more comfort with disclosing errors and accidents. The heightened transparency actually led to substantial safety improvements at Children's over time.

Heightened tolerance of failure not only surfaces errors that have already occurred; it encourages experimentation to increase the pace of problem-finding. As the employees at leading industrial design firm IDEO say, "Fail early and often to succeed sooner."[15] When people engage in low-cost, rapid experiments, they do not immediately discover the perfect course of action for the future. Instead, they gradually identify all the ideas that will *not* work, all the problems that can derail a particular strategy or initiative. As my colleague Amy Edmondson says, "It's the principle of the scientific method that you can only disconfirm, never confirm, a hypothesis."[16] Over time, many failed experiments enable us to discover what *will* work. Too often, though, companies only seem to encourage pilots and trials that aim to confirm what executives already believe, rather than to determine what will not work.

The Wharton School's Paul Schoemaker and his coauthor Robert Gunther argue that firms should design some low-cost experiments in which the probability and expectation of failure is relatively high. They describe these types of experiments as "deliberate mistakes." In these instances, managers seek to validate (or disconfirm) key assumptions before moving forward with a broader initiative. They deliberately set out to prove what could go wrong.[17]

Capital One, the credit card company, does not rely strictly on publicly available credit scores to evaluate potential customers; after all, each of its rivals has that same information. Instead, it conducts thousands of controlled experiments each year. Each experiment sets out to test a particular hypothesis about the factors that affect individual risk profiles. Undoubtedly, some of its mailings induce "bad risks" to sign up for a credit card. Capital One will lose money on those customers, and on some tests overall. In that sense, those experiments might be described as failures. However, each of these tests helps the company refine its proprietary algorithms that aim to predict the creditworthiness of each consumer. CEO and cofounder Richard Fairbank argues that the long-run profitability of the business rises as these algorithms become more accurate. Indeed, for many years, these algorithms provided Capital One with an ability to attract "good risks" and avoid "bad risks" more effectively than many rivals. Today, many of its rivals have emulated the firm's strategy of experimentation.[18]

Intolerance of failure diminishes problem-finding capabilities in one other important way. If we reassign or dismiss individuals soon after every failure, we lose valuable learning opportunities. The people responsible for a mistake often know the most about what went wrong and how to fix it moving forward. If we ostracize or dismiss these people, we lose their voices in the learning process. Perhaps the blame game drives out learning.

In some organizations, people want to forget failure as soon as possible; they do not reflect on those situations because it's painful and uncomfortable to do so. They prefer to learn from their past successes. However, we often attribute our successes to the wrong factors. We reduce a situation of complex causality to a simple story of how a particular decision led to an effective outcome. Scholars Philippe Baumard and William Starbuck have argued that "As it is often unclear whether a sequence of events adds up to success or failure, organization members slant interpretations to their own benefit."[19] We certainly discount the role of luck in many instances; we prefer to attribute good outcomes to our intelligence and thoughtful planning. Baumard and Starbuck conclude that "Research about learning from success says many firms improve their performance, but firms can over-learn the behaviors that they believe foster success and they become unrealistically confident that success will ensue."[20]

Learning from failures has its own shortcomings, though. People responsible for failures often try to present themselves in a positive light during many postmortems, and thereby distort what actually happened. A phenomenon known as "the fundamental attribution error" inhibits effective learning. By that, psychologists mean that we often attribute others' failures to their personal shortcomings, while explaining away our own errors as an outcome of unforeseeable external factors.[21] To identify the true problems in our organizations, we need to make people comfortable with admitting their own mistakes while avoiding pointing their finger at others. We have to lead by example, acknowledging our own missteps as leaders. When we talk about giving people "the freedom to fail," we have to be willing to back up our words with actions. Figuratively speaking, we must be willing to hold weekly meetings in a museum that features our past fiascoes, as well as our successes.

Acceptable Versus Unacceptable Failures

Does this mean that leaders should tolerate all failures? Of course not! Failures come in many shapes and sizes. Some failures may be tolerated; others should not be. Most executives do not have a clear set of criteria for differentiating the unacceptable failures from the ones that may be useful learning opportunities. The lack of clarity leaves employees unsure how they will be treated if they try something new and fail. The uncertainty regarding what constitutes a "blameworthy act" serves to suppress risk-taking, even when senior leaders have strongly expressed their desire not to punish people who fail.[22]

How, then, does one distinguish failures that are more acceptable from those that are far more inexcusable? Leaders need to examine how individuals behaved *before, during, and after* the failure (as shown in Figure 6.1). They have to understand the decision-making process that led to a particular course of action. They must examine how people reacted and adapted as the plan veered off course. Finally, leaders need to evaluate how individuals behaved in the aftermath of the failure, particularly the extent to which they accepted

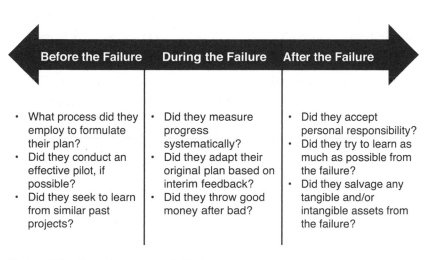

Before the Failure	During the Failure	After the Failure
• What process did they employ to formulate their plan? • Did they conduct an effective pilot, if possible? • Did they seek to learn from similar past projects?	• Did they measure progress systematically? • Did they adapt their original plan based on interim feedback? • Did they throw good money after bad?	• Did they accept personal responsibility? • Did they try to learn as much as possible from the failure? • Did they salvage any tangible and/or intangible assets from the failure?

Figure 6.1   How to assess a failure

responsibility for their mistakes and tried to learn from them. Perhaps most importantly, leaders need to communicate to the entire organization their criteria for distinguishing between tolerable and inexcusable failures.[23]

Before the Failure

When evaluating a failure, leaders need to examine the decision-making process employed by the key players. My research, as well as the studies conducted by other scholars, has identified certain attributes of high-quality decision-making processes. These characteristics do not guarantee that a good outcome will result, but they raise the probability substantially. In an effective decision-making process, groups generate and evaluate multiple alternatives. They surface and test key assumptions. Groups gather information that disconfirms existing views, not simply data that support the conventional wisdom. They gather information from a wide variety of sources, striving to find unbiased experts who can provide a fresh perspective. Effective teams engage in a vigorous debate while keeping the conflict constructive. Leaders encourage the expression of dissenting views. They genuinely want to hear what others think, rather than simply engaging in what management scholar Michael Watkins calls a "charade of consultation."[24] Effective teams consider worst-case scenarios and develop contingency plans. Ultimately, leaders should build commitment and shared understanding before moving forward with implementation. When examining a failure, you need to ask yourself: Did the key players employ a decision-making process with these attributes? Or did they fail to consider multiple options, quash dissenting views, and gather information in a biased way? If so, you should be much more cautious about excusing the failure.[25]

What else should we consider when evaluating a failure? We need to understand how goals were established at the outset of the project. Did the leader of the initiative establish a clear set of objectives and communicate those effectively to everyone involved in the implementation effort? When multiple goals exist, project leaders must make their priorities clear so that others know how to make trade-offs if necessary as the effort unfolds. Moreover, one should look for evidence of clear metrics and milestones that were established to track progress against the goals over time.

We should examine too whether a project's leaders conducted appropriate prototyping and/or pilot studies before implementing their course of action. Did they conduct a test of modest cost and risk before diving headfirst into a massive rollout of the project? Did they design a good pilot, or did they stack the deck to get the result that they desired? During my research, one retailer explained why a recent pilot of a new concept had proven problematic when conducted in a handful of the chain's stores. Senior managers at the corporate office "held the stores' hands" during the pilot, working alongside the store management team and the associates each day. The corporate officers wanted to make the pilot as successful as possible. Given that interventionist behavior, the pilot proved to be a very poor test of whether this concept could be rolled out effectively throughout the chain. Thus, one should always ask not only *if* a pilot was conducted, but *how* it was performed.

Finally, we ought to consider whether a project's leaders tried to learn from past successes and failures before embarking on their chosen course of action. Did they repeat past missteps? If so, did those mistakes occur because the project's leaders failed to examine the best and worst practices of the past? Did they fail to learn from history?

During the Failure

Failures certainly should be deemed inexcusable if a project's leaders violate the organization's values and principles or, worse yet, break the law during the implementation process. Beyond identifying such egregious behaviors, we should examine whether a project's leaders measured progress systematically. Did they gather feedback from multiple voices and assess progress against the original goals and objectives on a regular basis? As negative feedback emerged, or external conditions changed, did the project's leaders adapt their original plan? We would like to see evidence of real-time learning and adjustments.

At some point, though, a project's leaders should at least consider cutting their losses. In assessing a failure, one must ask: Did individuals "throw good money after bad" in this situation? Too often individuals allow the size of past investments to affect their decision regarding whether to move forward with a course of action, even if those investments are irrecoverable. Prior investments represent sunk costs, which should be irrelevant to current choices regarding whether to move forward with a project. However, research shows that individuals tend to pursue activities in which they have made substantial prior investments. Often, they become overly committed to certain activities despite consistently poor results. As a result, individuals make additional investments in the hopes of achieving a successful turnaround. They escalate their commitment to a deteriorating situation.

Several experimental studies have demonstrated that people fail to ignore sunk costs when making investment decisions. For instance, Barry Staw's 1976 study represents one of the first laboratory experiments aimed at testing the sunk-cost effect.[26] Staw assigned business students the role of a senior corporate manager in charge of allocating resources to various business units. One half of the subjects made an initial resource allocation and received feedback on their decision. Then the subjects made a second resource allocation to the business units. The other half of the subjects did not make the initial allocation. Instead, they received information about the previous allocation, along with feedback.

Staw found that the subjects who made the initial investment decision themselves chose to allocate a higher dollar amount in the second period than those who did not make the initial allocation. In addition, Staw gave one half of the students positive feedback regarding the initial allocation, while the other half received negative feedback. Subjects allocated more dollars to the poorly performing business units than to successful ones. This supported the prediction that individuals would commit additional resources to unsuccessful activities in order to justify past actions.

Do real managers make similar mistakes, just as these students did in the laboratory? Staw and his colleague, Ha Hoang, decided to find out. They collected information on National Basketball Association (NBA) draft picks over a seven-year period.[27] Staw and Hoang argued that draft order should not predict playing time in the NBA, after controlling for productivity, unless management has allowed sunk costs to shape their decisions. In other words, a number-one draft pick should not garner more playing time than the twenty-fifth pick in the draft if both players have performed equally well in the NBA up to that point in time. The study's results indicate that sunk costs do matter. The players' draft order affects playing time, length of service in the league, and the probability of being traded by their initial team. These effects hold even when controlling for actual performance in the league. In other words, when making decisions, management and coaches tend to overweigh the fact that they have expended a great deal of resources for a particular player. They continue investing in that player for years in hopes of justifying their past expenditures. They throw good playing time after bad.[28]

One might argue that a study of basketball players does not prove that business executives have a hard time cutting their losses. In fact, research shows that people in all fields, including business, have a hard time ignoring sunk costs. As a classic example, consider the construction of the Concorde, the commercial supersonic jet built in the 1970s. As you may recall, the Concorde flew between Europe and the United States for twenty-seven years, making the trip at record speeds—half the time it took a commercial airliner to travel from Paris to New York. In the relatively early stages of that project, it became quite clear that it had virtually no chance of being a financial success. British and French business and political leaders nearly canceled the project. However, they chose to plow ahead, arguing that they did not want to "waste" the vast amount of resources that already had been expended. Ultimately, the cost of developing the Concorde exceeded the original budget by 500%. The investment never yielded a positive financial return.[29]

Given overwhelming evidence that human beings are susceptible to the sunk-cost effect, we must look out for this phenomenon when examining failures. We have to examine the evidence to determine whether managers expressed concern about wasting prior investments, and thus poured additional funds into a failing project. Yes, persistence can be valuable. Sometimes, we want our managers to push through obstacles; no one likes a quitter, as they say. However, we must be concerned if someone ignores all advice and evidence to the contrary and continues to throw good money after bad. We certainly should be wary if an individual or team appears to have a track record indicating a reticence to cut their losses when projects go south.

After the Failure

What about a manager's behavior after a failure? How should one assess that conduct to determine whether a failure should be deemed tolerable versus inexcusable? To begin, a project leader needs to take responsibility for his or her mistakes. This person cannot point fingers at others and dodge accountability. Former Secretary of State Robert McNamara shared an interesting story with me about President John F. Kennedy in the aftermath of the Bay of Pigs fiasco. Kennedy told his advisers that he would address the nation on television, at which time he would say, "The buck stops here. I was responsible. It was a miserable failure. Success has many fathers. Failure has none. But, in this case, I am the father, and it was my failure." McNamara recalls that he offered to appear on television shortly after Kennedy's speech. He would explain that the entire Cabinet bore responsibility, because none of its members had objected to the invasion plans. They had given the president poor advice and counsel. McNamara recalls being rebuffed by Kennedy. The president replied, "No, no, Bob. It was my responsibility. I didn't have to take the advice. I have to stand up and take responsibility."[30] We would like to see similar behavior on the part of managers in our organizations who have been responsible for failures. We do not want them to deflect blame to their team; we want them to acknowledge that they made the ultimate decisions.

In the aftermath of failures, we also should expect to see managers conducting a systematic "after-action review."[31] They should be willing to bring in outside, unbiased facilitators to help lead that postmortem analysis. The managers should not only derive learning from the incident for themselves; they should actively try to share that learning with others throughout the organization. They need to be willing to help others avoid making the same mistakes again.

Last, we should examine whether managers tried to salvage certain assets, both tangible and intangible, in the wake of the failure. Did they harvest the project for valuable resources that might be exploited elsewhere in the organization? Pharmaceutical companies now systematically examine past research projects that ended in failure, hoping to find other uses for the drug. For instance, at Eli Lilly, the company's leadership team "assigns someone—often a team of doctors and scientists—to retrospectively analyze every compound that has failed at any point in human clinical trials."[32] According to the *Wall Street Journal*, many Eli Lilly products have emerged from an analysis of prior failed research efforts. Consider Evista, a popular drug for osteoporosis, which now generates more than $1 billion in revenue per year for the company. That drug emerged from a failed research project aimed at developing a new contraceptive.[33] Managers at all companies should mine their failures in hopes of salvaging intellectual property, as well as physical assets, which may be valuable in other uses moving forward.

Useful, Low-Cost Failures

To close the chapter, let us consider the attitude toward failure at one of the world's most creative companies—Pixar Animation Studios. Many people marvel at the success of Pixar, creators of blockbuster movies such as *Toy Story* and *Finding Nemo*. The company's origins trace back to 1984, when John Lasseter left Disney to join filmmaker George Lucas's computer graphics group. Two years later, Steve Jobs acquired this unit from Lucas for $10 million, and it became known as Pixar. For years, the company produced award-winning short films (known as shorts) as well as commercials. Then, in 1995, Pixar released its first feature film; *Toy Story* became the highest-grossing film in the nation and received several Academy Award nominations. A string of critically acclaimed and financially successful feature films followed. Meanwhile, Disney's vaunted animation studios languished. Disney acquired its principal rival, Pixar, for $7.4 billion in 2006. After the deal closed, the Pixar team took the lead in trying to reinvigorate the Disney studios.[34]

Randy Nelson serves as the dean of Pixar University—the company's educational and developmental program for its employees. Nelson helps employees learn how to become better animators. He wants them to view "art as a team sport"—that is, he hopes they will see that the best, most creative films are products of collaboration, not simply individual genius.[35] To do so, he brings employees into classes where they "make art together and flop publicly."[36] During a session, Nelson puts each illustration on the wall. Then he critiques each person's work in front of his or her peers. He believes that constructive feedback is essential to producing great work; people must learn to take risks, listen to critiques, and improve their work. "You need an environment to foster risk-taking and error recovery," says Nelson. "You have to honor failure because failure is just the negative space around success."[37]

Pixar believes strongly in honoring failure, as well reminding everyone that even the most creative and successful animators get it wrong at times. As you walk through the halls at Pixar, you see many sketches that were cut from various films.[38] These creative failures remind everyone that truly creative and innovative risk-takers will fail on more than one occasion. The walls serve a purpose similar to the fiascoes displayed in Alessi's museum.

Pixar also understands the value of rapid, relatively low-cost experimentation. It knows that reducing the time and expense associated with a mistake makes failure that much more palatable. For this reason, Lasseter has restarted the production of animated shorts at Walt Disney Studios—a practice that had occurred only sparingly in recent years. Throughout Pixar's history, Lasseter and others have used shorts as a mechanism to experiment with and refine various computer animation techniques. Interestingly, Walt Disney built his studio in the 1930s based on a series of popular shorts, earning ten Academy Awards for them between 1932 and 1942.

Don Hahn, producer of *The Lion King*, points out that "Shorts have always been a wellspring of techniques, ideas, and young talent."[39] Now, it seems that Lasseter is returning Disney animation to its roots in hopes of rekindling the creativity that, once upon a time, made the Disney animators the envy of the entertainment world.

Lasseter has asked young talent at the studio to direct these five-minute shorts. The budget for a short represents less than 2% of the money required to fund a major animated film. It costs $2 million or less to produce a five-minute short, while the expense for a feature film often runs well over $100 million.[40] Chuck Williams, a veteran story artist at the company, commented on the program:

> "They allow you to develop new talent. Shorts are your farm team, where the new directors and art directors are going to come from. Instead of taking a chance on an $80 million feature with a first-time director, art director or head of story, you can spend a fraction of that on a short and see what they can do.[41]

Already, Lasseter's program has identified someone with the potential to direct a feature film. After watching a quirky five-minute short titled *Glago's Guest*, Lasseter chose its director, Chris Williams, to take over as the director on *Bolt*—a Disney computer-animated film released in November 2008. Williams had never directed a feature film, but Lasseter used the five-minute short as training ground for him.[42]

With this program, Lasseter has deployed a relatively small amount of capital, yet provided talented up-and-comers an opportunity to try their hand at directing their first animated film. The cost of a failure is quite low. He can encourage young talent to take risks without worrying about a huge financial loss in the case of a failure. The time required to conduct these experiments also is quite low—shorts do not take years to produce. Some shorts will not work out. Through the development process, however, Lasseter and his team will identify the techniques and practices that do not work as effectively as they should at the Disney studio. They will find the problems that have hindered Disney's success over the past decade. Moreover, they will identify people who may not be strong enough to direct feature-length films.

Other firms should take notice. They should look for their own low-risk, low-cost opportunities to spark innovation and creativity, while simultaneously developing and evaluating young, talented employees. After all, when failures are costly, no leader wants to tolerate them. The most useful failures enable us to learn quickly and inexpensively.

Endnotes

[1] For extensive details on James Dyson and the history of the firm that bears his name, see the company's website: http://www.dyson.com/about/story/.

[2] Vorasarun, C. "Clean machine." *Forbes*. March 24, 2008.

[3] Clark, H. "James Dyson cleans up." *Forbes*. August 1, 2006.

[4] Ibid.

[5] Salter, C. "Failure doesn't suck." *Fast Company*. May 2007.

[6] Ibid.

[7] Wylie, I. "Failure is glorious." *Fast Company*. September 2001.

[8] Kamenev, M. "Alessi: Fun design for everyone." *Business Week*. July 25, 2006.

[9] http://executiveeducation.wharton.upenn.edu/ebuzz/0508/fellows.html.

[10] Wylie, I. (2001).

[11] http://cxccutivccducation.wharton.upenn.edu/ebuzz/0508/fellows.html.

[12] Wylie, I. (2001).

[13] I have published a case study about Children's Hospital and Clinics of Minneapolis, along with my coauthors Amy Edmondson and Anita Tucker, based on a series of interviews with leaders at that hospital. Edmondson, A., M. Roberto, and A. Tucker. (2002). "Children's Hospital and Clinics (A)." Harvard Business School Case Study No. 9-302-050. This section also benefits from my time spent with Julie Morath and Dr. Chris Robison when they visited my class during the first occasion on which I taught the case study to MBA students. A supplemental case also has been written, helping inform students how the patient safety initiative evolved from 2002 to 2007. See Edmondson, A., K. Roloff, and I. Nembhard. (2007). "Children's Hospital and Clinics (B)." Harvard Business School Case Study No. 9-608-073. For more information about Children's patient safety efforts, see also Shapiro, J. "Taking the mistakes out of medicine." *U.S. News and World Report*. July 17, 2000.

[14] Edmondson, A., M. Roberto, and A. Tucker. (2002).

[15] Kelley, T. (2001). *The Art of Innovation: Lessons in Creativity from IDEO, America's Leading Design Firm*. New York: Doubleday. p. 232.

[16] McGregor, J. "How failure breeds success." *Business Week*. July 10, 2006.

[17] Schoemaker, P. and R. Gunther. (2006). "The wisdom of deliberate mistakes." *Harvard Business Review*. June: 108–115.

[18] This section draws from a case study about Capital One that is taught in many strategy courses. See Anand, B., M. Rukstad, and C. Paige. (2000). "Capital One Financial Corp." Harvard Business School Case Study No. 9-700-124. In addition, this section benefits from what I learned when Capital One CEO Richard Fairbank visited my class in 2001.

[19] Baumard, P. and W. Starbuck. (2005). "Learning from failures: Why it may not happen." *Long Range Planning*. 38: 281–298. This quote appears on pages 283–284.

[20] Baumard, P. and W. Starbuck. (2005). p. 282.

[21] Ross, L. (1977). "The intuitive psychologist and his shortcomings: Distortions in the attribution process." In L. Berkowitz (ed.). *Advances in Experimental Social Psychology* (vol. 10, pp. 173–220). New York: Academic Press.

[22] For more on tolerating failure, as well as the types of questions that leaders should consider when evaluating failures, see Farson, R. and R. Keyes. (2002). "The failure-tolerant leader." *Harvard Business Review*. August: 64–71.

[23] Sim Sitkin defines intelligent failures as those that provide bountiful opportunities for learning and improvement. In that sense, they are perhaps not only excusable, but, to some extent, desirable for the organization. Sitkin identifies several attributes

of intelligent failures: carefully planned action, uncertain outcomes, modest scale and scope, executed efficiently, and familiar territory where learning can easily take place. See Sitkin, S. B. (1996). "Learning through failure: The strategy of small losses." In M. D. Cohen and L. S. Sproull (eds.). *Organizational Learning* (pp. 541–578). Thousand Oaks, CA: Sage.

[24] Personal conversations with Michael Watkins, professor at the Institute for Management Development (IMD) in Lausanne, Switzerland.

[25] For an examination of my research on decision-making processes, see Roberto, M. (2005). *Why Great Leaders Don't Take Yes for an Answer: Managing for Conflict and Consensus*. Upper Saddle River, NJ: Wharton School Publishing. That book contains many citations to academic articles I have written regarding the attributes of high-quality decision processes. In addition, one should examine the work of scholars such as Kathleen Eisenhardt and Irving Janis. For instance, see Janis, I. (1989). *Crucial Decisions*. New York: Free Press; Bourgeois, L. J. and K. Eisenhardt. (1988). "Strategic decision processes in high velocity environments: Four cases in the microcomputer industry." *Management Science*. 34: 816–835; Dean, J. and M. Sharfman. (1996). "Does decision process matter?" *Academy of Management Journal*. 39: 368–396. For a review of studies in this area, see Rajagopalan, N., A. Rasheed, and D. Datta. (1993). "Strategic decision processes: Critical review and future directions." *Journal of Management*. 19: 349–364.

[26] Staw, B. M. (1976). "Knee deep in the big muddy: A study of escalating commitment to a chosen course of action." *Organizational Behavior and Human Performance*. 16: 27–44.

[27] Staw, B. M. and H. Hoang. (1995). "Sunk costs in the NBA: Why draft order affects playing time and survival in professional basketball." *Administrative Science Quarterly*. 40: 474–494.

[28] For additional studies on the sunk-cost effect, see the following: Arkes, H. R and C. Blumer. (1985). "The psychology of sunk cost." *Organizational Behavior and Human Decision Processes*. 35: 124–140; Brockner, J. (1992). "The escalation of commitment to a failing course of action: Toward theoretical progress." *Academy of Management Review*. 17(1): 39–61.

[29] http://www.concordesst.com/history/eh5.html#n.

[30] Former Secretary of Defense Robert McNamara told this story to me and my students when he visited my class in the spring of 2005.

[31] David Garvin has written extensively on the topic of after-action reviews, as conducted by the U.S. Army. See Garvin, D. (2000). *Learning in Action: A Guide to Putting the Learning Organization to Work*. Boston: Harvard Business School Press.

[32] Burton, T. "Flop factor: by learning from failures." *Wall Street Journal*. April 21, 2004. p. A1.

[33] Ibid.

[34] For a complete history of Pixar Animation Studios, see Price, D. (2008). *The Pixar Touch: The Making of a Company*. New York: Knopf.

[35] Bunn, A. "Welcome to Planet Pixar." *Wired*. December 2006.

[36] Sanders, A. "Brainstorm Zone." *San Francisco Business Times*. May 6, 2005.

[37] Bunn, A. (2006).

[38] Sanders, A. (2005).

[39] Solomon, C. "For Disney, something old (and short) is new again." *New York Times*. December 3, 2006.

[40] Grover, R. "Disney bets long on film shorts." *Business Week*. May 4, 2007.

[41] Solomon, C. (2006).

[42] Grover, R. (2007).

7

Teach How to Talk and Listen

"It's not what you tell them...it's what they hear."
—Arnold "Red" Auerbach

On March 27, 1977 five hundred eighty-three people died in the worst accident in aviation history. Two Boeing 747 planes collided that day at Los Rodeos Airport on Tenerife in the Canary Islands. KLM Flight 4805 originated from Amsterdam, and Pan Am Flight 1736 had begun in Los Angeles. Each plane intended to land at Las Palmas, the larger of the two airports in the Canary Islands. However, a terrorist bombing that day had closed Las Palmas, causing flights to be diverted to Tenerife, a much smaller airport not well-suited to serve jumbo jets.[1]

Jacob Veldhuyzen van Zanten piloted the KLM flight, which carried two hundred thirty-four passengers and fourteen crew members. Van Zanten had worked for KLM since 1947. The company featured him in its advertising, including in the issue of its in-flight magazine onboard that day. He was the head of the airline's flight training program, and he trained many of KLM's other pilots and copilots. In this role, he had spent much more time recently in the simulator than flying charter or commercial flights. Prior to this particular flight, van Zanten had worked exclusively in the simulator for twelve weeks. He had trained the copilot during this time.

Captain Victor Grubbs piloted the Pan Am flight, which carried three hundred eighty passengers and sixteen crew members. The

139

plane represented a slice of aviation history, since it was the first Boeing 747 jet to fly passengers (in January 1970). Grubbs landed at 2:15 that afternoon, roughly one half-hour after the KLM jet arrived at Tenerife. The small airport had limited taxi space, so Grubbs had to park behind the KLM jet. Several other large jets also diverted to Tenerife, which became increasingly crowded.

While waiting for the Las Palmas airport to reopen, Captain van Zanten decided to refuel his plane. He made this decision due to concerns about Dutch law, which had specific restrictions on flight and duty time for crews. The pilot knew that his crew was quite close to its monthly limits. Van Zanten worried that the crew would exceed these legal limits if they did not depart from Las Palmas by seven o'clock that evening. Therefore, he chose to refuel on Tenerife so that he could take advantage of the idle time sitting on the tarmac and then execute a rapid turnaround at Las Palmas. As it turned out, the Las Palmas airport reopened at 2:30 p.m. The Pan Am jet wanted to depart, but it could not get around the KLM plane at the small airport. Refueling took several hours, during which time the Pan Am plane remained parked behind the KLM jet. As the planes sat on the runway, the weather worsened considerably. Visibility became very limited, as low as 300 meters in some locations.

At 4:56 p.m., air traffic controllers directed the KLM jet to proceed down the takeoff runway, perform a 180-degree turn, and await clearance for takeoff. The KLM jet conducted the turn, a rather complex maneuver given the tight space. The controllers asked the Pan Am crew to follow the KLM plane down the runway, take the third exit onto a parallel taxiway, and then come around behind the KLM jet to be next in line for takeoff. The Pan Am crew tried to follow these instructions, but they became confused. Visibility had deteriorated, and the runway exits lacked clear signage. Moreover, the third exit required a very tight 135-degree turn, unlike the more easily navigable 45-degree angle at the fourth exit. For these reasons, the Pan

Am crew missed the third exit and continued heading toward the fourth one.

Meanwhile, van Zanten began to throttle his engines, and the plane began to move ahead. Klaus Meurs, the copilot, expressed surprise. He said, "Wait. We don't have clearance!"[2] Van Zanten asked Meurs to obtain clearance for takeoff from the air traffic controllers. The KLM pilot clearly seemed to be in a bit of a hurry to get off the ground, given his concerns about Dutch restrictions on crew flight time. Meurs requested clearance, but the air traffic controllers responded with instructions regarding what to do after the plane had become airborne. The controllers did not provide takeoff clearance, but they did use the word "takeoff" as part of their instructions. Meurs confirmed the details about what to do after becoming airborne, though he did not confirm explicitly that the KLM jet had clearance for takeoff. While Meurs spoke, van Zanten throttled the engines and began to move forward again. Meurs closed his statement with the ambiguous phrase "We're now at takeoff." The air traffic controllers, as well as the Pan Am crew, believed that this statement meant the KLM plane was in ready position at the end of the runway, *awaiting clearance for takeoff.* The controller responded, "OK. Stand by for takeoff. I will call you." The Pan Am crew responded firmly, "We are still taxiing down the runway." Unfortunately, these important statements became difficult, but not completely impossible, to hear inside the KLM jet because of radio interference that impeded clear transmission. Meanwhile, the Pan Am plane had not yet reached the fourth exit.

At this point, the air traffic controllers asked the Pan Am crew to report when they had exited the runway. The Pan Am crew replied, "OK. We will report when we are clear." The KLM flight engineer, William Schreuder, heard this exchange and became concerned. He asked van Zanten rather tentatively, "Did he not clear the runway, then?" The captain responded, "What do you say?" Schreuder asked again, "Is he not clear, that Pan American?" The captain heard and understood the awkward question, and he replied emphatically, "Oh yes." He believed that the runway was clear, and he proceeded with takeoff. Schreuder did not question the captain any further. First officer Meurs also offered no objection. Because of the extremely low visibility, the KLM crew could not see the Pan Am jet ahead of them on the runway.

Inside the Pan Am cockpit, the crew discussed van Zanten's apparent anxiousness to depart. Captain Grubbs said, "Let's get the hell out of here." Flight engineer George Warns noted that van Zanten appeared anxious and said, "After he's held us up for all this time, now he's in a rush." Moments later, the Pan Am crew noticed the KLM jet headed right toward them. Grubbs yelled, "There he is...look at him! Goddamn, that son of a bitch is coming!" Copilot Robert Bragg shouted, "Get off! Get off! Get off!" Grubbs tried feverishly to turn off the runway.

At the very last moment, van Zanten saw the Pan Am jet on the runaway in front of him and tried to avoid the crash. The KLM jet became airborne, but its fuselage scraped the top off the Pan Am plane during liftoff. The KLM jet slammed back into the ground, killing everyone onboard. The Pan Am plane burst into flames. Only fifty-six passengers and five crew members survived.

What went so terribly wrong in this case? Clearly, the crowded conditions at the small airport, poor weather, air traffic control's lack of experience in working with 747 jets, and the KLM pilot's anxiousness to depart all contributed to the disaster. Beyond that, though, University of Michigan Professor Karl Weick argues that "The Tenerife disaster was built out of a series of small, semi-standardized misunderstandings."[3] For instance, much confusion surrounded the use of the word "takeoff" during communications between the controllers and the KLM crew. Air traffic control never believed that it had granted clearance for takeoff. The Pan Am crew also did not believe that clearance had been given. Throughout the communication, the parties did not always seek or provide confirmation from each other in unambiguous terms; they used casual, nonstandard language at times. People assumed the consent of others without adequate verification. Moreover, van Zanten had spent a great deal of time in the simulator, where a training pilot often issues takeoff clearance himself, rather than communicating with air traffic control, as on a normal flight. Thus, van Zanten may not have been recently accustomed to seeking and receiving confirmation on key communications.

The evidence suggests that the culture of the cockpit contributed to the tragedy as well. The copilot and the flight engineer demonstrated a great deal of deference to the captain, as was customary at the time. Neither one spoke up as forcefully as they could have to question the captain's decision to commence takeoff. Weick argues that stress often causes hierarchy and authority to become more salient to people. In other words, as the stress levels rose during that afternoon, the KLM crew behaved less and less as a team of equals. Open communication and candid dialogue suffered as a result. Weick describes the condition in the cockpit during those final moments before the crash as pluralistic ignorance. He explains, "Pluralistic ignorance applied to an incipient crisis means I am puzzled by what is going on, but I assume no one else is, especially because they have more experience, more seniority, higher rank."[4] In those final moments, he posits that the other crew members may have been thinking, "Surely the captain knows that the runway may not be clear."[5]

Crew Resource Management Training

During the 1970s, aviation safety experts became quite concerned after a series of major accidents such as the Tenerife tragedy. The National Aeronautics and Space Administration (NASA) hosted a workshop on aviation safety in 1979 to discuss this issue. Research presented at this workshop demonstrated that mechanical failure did not represent the principal cause of air transport accidents. More-over, most crashes did not occur because the crew lacked the appropriate technical skills and capabilities. The researchers focused instead on *deficiencies related to interpersonal communication, teamwork, decision-making, and leadership.* The workshop participants identified the need for a training program to develop these cognitive and interpersonal skills. Airlines began to implement Crew Resource Management (CRM) training in the years that followed.[6] More recently, others have adopted this approach, including the military, the merchant navy, the nuclear power industry, firefighters, health care organizations, and offshore oil and gas companies. Many organizations have reported substantial safety improvements as a result of applying CRM techniques.[7]

CRM strove to change the culture of flight crews. Robert Helmreich and Clayton Foushee described the ethos of pilots in decades past:

> "In the early years, the image of a pilot was of a single, stalwart individual, white scarf trailing, braving the elements in an open cockpit. This stereotype embraces a number of personality traits such as independence, machismo, bravery, and calmness under stress that are more associated with individual activity than with team effort... Indeed, in 1952 the guidelines for proficiency checks at one major airline categorically stated that the first officer should not correct errors made by the captain."[8]

The captain possessed tremendous authority and status. The crew learned not to question the pilot's judgment. According to Robert Ginnett of the Center for Creative Leadership, a humorous sign found on the bulletin board of a commercial airline revealed fundamental attitudes regarding the crew's relationship with the captain. The sign read: "The two rules of commercial aviation—Rule 1: The captain is ALWAYS right. Rule 2: See Rule 1."[9]

CRM set out to change the culture and attitudes of flight crews. The training emphasized teamwork over individualism, and it focused on interpersonal communication skills. Copilots and flight engineers learned how to be assertive, yet respectful, when they believed that a situation had become unsafe. Captains learned to invite input from other crew members, beginning with the statements they made during the preflight briefing. Ginnett describes how one highly effective captain spoke to his crew: "I just want you guys to understand that they assign the seats in this airplane based on seniority, not on the basis of competence. So anything you can see or do that will help out, I'd sure appreciate hearing about it."[10]

Chapter 1, "From Problem-Solving to Problem-Finding," mentioned that Captain Al Haynes attributed the remarkable emergency landing of United Flight 232 in Sioux City, Iowa to the crew's CRM training. In a speech to NASA two years after that incident, Haynes said:

> "The preparation that paid off for the crew was something that United started in 1980 called Cockpit Resource Management... All the other airlines are now using it. Up until 1980, we kind of worked on the concept that the captain was THE authority on the aircraft. What he said, goes. And we lost a few airplanes because of that. Sometimes the captain isn't as smart as we thought he was... Why would I know more about getting that airplane on the ground under those conditions than the other three (crew members)? So, if I hadn't used CRM, if we had not let everybody put their input in, it's a cinch we wouldn't have made it."[11]

The following sections describe some of the key cognitive and interpersonal skills involved in CRM and explain how any organization can develop its employee capabilities in these areas. To begin, it helps to teach people about the types of communication errors that commonly take place.

Communication Errors

The International Association of Fire Chiefs (IAFC) has developed a detailed document for describing how firefighters can adopt

CRM practices.[12] In that work, they identify errors that people sending and receiving messages often make. Sender errors include omitting key information and/or providing biased information. Omissions may occur because the speaker is in a hurry, or perhaps he or she has made assumptions about what the listener already knows. Senders also make the mistake of ignoring the impact of nonverbal cues such as body language, facial expressions, eye contact, and gestures. Senders may speak too quickly, not giving the listeners time to digest what they have heard and to ask clarifying questions. When I was learning to teach, Professor Martin Feldstein once advised me, "You have to be comfortable with silence on occasion when you lecture. Students need time to formulate questions or craft responses to your queries."[13] Along these same lines, speakers often forget to vary their tempo; slowing down and/or changing one's intonation can help emphasize key ideas. Senders sometimes forget to repeat important messages; they assume that others heard and understood them the first time they described a thought or made a suggestion. Finally, speakers often assume that silence equals assent; when others do not object to a particular statement or request, we automatically conclude that they must support us.

Individuals receiving messages make a number of mistakes that impede effective communication as well. Often we make up our minds before others have spoken. Sometimes we begin thinking about how to respond before the speaker has completed his or her thought. We make many assumptions about the meanings of particular words and ideas, often jumping to the conclusion that the speaker is employing the same language system to which we are accustomed. We attribute the wrong intent to others' messages, perhaps because that helps us explain to ourselves why they disagree with our views. Receivers miss nonverbal signals, just as senders often underemphasize their importance. Listeners fail to ask for clarification and confirmation. As we saw in the Tenerife disaster, confirming what you have heard proves critical at times to avoid serious misunderstandings. Finally, receivers often choose to multitask, causing them not to hear key words and statements. As you watch a management meeting in which everyone keeps checking their personal digital assistants under the table, you know that communication breakdowns are quite likely to occur.[14]

Improving Interpersonal Communication

How, then, can we improve communication within our organizations so that we do not have leaders and team members behaving as the crew did during the Tenerife disaster? Leaders clearly must change their own behavior and improve their own communication with others. Moreover, organizational leaders must become teachers; they have to take responsibility for developing the interpersonal communication skills of their subordinates. If necessary, leaders may bring in outside experts, as the airlines have done with CRM trainers. Above all else, senior leaders must model good behavior for everyone else in the enterprise.

To begin, we must focus on the importance of that first meeting when a team comes together to launch a project. That meeting represents an opportunity to begin the team formation process—to clarify goals, norms, and responsibilities. Airlines call these meetings "preflight briefings." We also should pay close attention to the "handoffs" that occur in our organizations—those times when a task or project passes from one unit of the enterprise to another. Problems often occur during these handoffs. Poor communication causes critical information to not pass from one group to another, and larger problems begin to build. Finally, leaders must take the responsibility to teach their people how to speak up assertively when they spot problems, as well as how to listen effectively when someone comes forward with bad news.

Briefings

As former U.S. Airways pilot Kelly Ison says, "good communication begins with an effective crew briefing before the first leg of a series of flights that we embark upon together over four or five days."[15] That briefing helps bring together the team, outline the shared goals and objectives, and establish the norms of behavior. Ison points out that many errors and near-misses happen on the first leg of the first day during which a crew flies together. Thus, he advocates the use of that briefing to build familiarity with one another and to clarify the team structure to avoid such mishaps.

The pilot ensures that everyone understands their roles and responsibilities during the preflight briefing.[16] The team reviews the timing and sequence of key tasks that must be accomplished, as well as the distribution of the workload among crew members. An effective briefing includes a discussion about the types of unplanned events that might occur, and how the team will approach these situations. Perhaps most importantly, Ison contends that the captain must open the avenues of communication during that briefing. For instance, Ison suggests that the pilot tell the crew, "Come to me if you see problems or unexpected events. I'm here and want to know if you believe a problem exists." Throughout the briefing, the team gets to know one another, and they begin practicing the communication techniques they will need to execute a successful flight.

Military aviators emphasize the critical importance of preflight briefings as well. Former F-15 pilot James Murphy argues that "The mission is the brief; the brief is the mission. The two are inextricably linked in that pilot's mind, and he or she would no more fly a mission without a brief than drive to work naked."[17] As you might expect from a soldier, Murphy argues that briefings should be precise. He explains that leaders should "chair-fly" the mission prior to a briefing in order for it to be successful. By chair flying, he means that the leader should sit down and visualize how the mission will unfold. Seek out potential flaws in the mission, as well as unplanned events that might affect the team. Anticipate questions that your team may ask you about the goals and plans for the mission. Murphy concludes, "I can't tell you how many times I realized there was a mistake in the execution phase by just chair-flying the mission before putting the briefing on."[18] Interestingly, people in other professions employ such visualization techniques prior to bringing a team together to accomplish a challenging goal. For instance, accomplished mountaineer David Breashears explains that he spends weeks before an expedition "envisioning every possible scenario that might unfold on the mountain."[19] Then he reviews key scenarios with his team at the outset of the expedition.

What's happening with these "chair-flying" activities? Murphy and Breashears have visualized potential problems and have shared these thoughts with their team. That up-front communication helps others spot those problems if they arise down the road. Chair-flying the mission and visualizing possible pitfalls sends a strong message to your team that you do not expect a perfect implementation process; you are prepared for a myriad of errors and disruptions. Having heard their leaders discuss these scenarios, individuals feel more comfortable coming forward later to surface a problem they have spotted.

Do companies launch projects in this manner? Clearly, they often do not. We bring together a group of talented people, and we expect them to perform well as a team. Like airline flight crews, we sometimes bring teams together whose members do not know one another, or who have not worked together on a regular basis. We do not always take the steps required to lay a solid foundation for that team at the outset.[20] Organizational teams need to develop their own version of the preflight briefing. They must use these launch meetings to clarify shared goals and norms, as well as each member's roles and responsibilities. Team members should discuss how they will communicate with one another, and the leader must take special care to establish an atmosphere of candid dialogue.

Handoffs

Health care organizations have discovered that effective "handoffs" prove critical to reducing medical accidents. Consider what happens when a patient has surgery. The operating team must hand off the patient to the group working in the postoperative recovery area. After some time, that group must hand off the patient to floor nurses who will care for the individual during his or her stay in one of the hospital's beds. Successful care of that patient requires that crucial information pass from one group to the other during this process. In the past, though, many medical accidents occurred because communication broke down; hospitals fumbled the handoffs.[21]

Today, hospitals work diligently to ensure that clear and concise briefings occur at the time of these handoffs. For instance, at Children's Hospital in Boston, the staff in the postsurgical recovery area calls the floor nurse prior to transferring the patient to a bed. The recovery nurse explains the individual's condition in detail. Then the recovery nurse typically accompanies the patient to his or her room and conducts an in-person briefing with the floor nurse. Together, they review the patient's chart and discuss what should take place moving forward. They also talk about what issues or problems might arise, and what the floor nurse should "keep an eye on" moving forward.[22]

Like these hospitals, business enterprises must think about where the critical handoffs take place in their organization. When and where do key projects and tasks shift from being the chief responsibility of one unit to another? What information is most likely to fall through the cracks? How should these briefings take place to ensure a smooth handoff?

A few simple communication strategies help make handoffs more successful. First, communicate face-to-face whenever possible, thereby enabling the use of nonverbal cues and interactive questioning. Second, provide written information in advance of the face-to-face meeting so that the receiving party can prepare for the handoff. Third, avoid interruptions while striving to keep the briefing as concise as possible. Fourth, bring teams together to brief one another, rather than relying on a representative from each group to execute the handoff; this reduces the potential for miscommunication by removing that extra step in the process. Finally, each party should confirm their interpretations of what they have heard.[23]

Speaking Up Effectively

Sometimes problems do not surface in organizations because individuals do not know how to speak up effectively. People try to communicate their concerns, but they cannot seem to get anyone to listen. They may pose a question quite tentatively, as the flight engineer did in the final moments of the Tenerife tragedy. Perhaps individuals manage to get the ear of a senior executive, but they fail to persuade. Leaders have a responsibility to coach and teach their people how to speak up assertively, yet respectfully, when they spot a problem or have a dissenting view. Speaking up requires skill, not just courage.

Crew Resource Management (CRM) expert Todd Bishop of the Error Prevention Institute has developed a five-step process for how to speak up assertively when you see a problem.[24] To begin, you should address the person to whom you are expressing your concerns by name. Then, you must express your concern concisely and clearly, using an "owned emotion." By that, Bishop means that you should explain how the problem has made you think and feel. Use the first person, rather than projecting your emotions onto others. For instance, you might say, "I have a bad feeling because..." State the problem as it appears to you: "From my perspective, it looks as if..." Next, be sure to propose one or more alternative solutions to the problem. As the old saying goes, "Don't tell me about the flood. Build me an ark." In this case, Bishop advocates describing why you perceive a flood taking place and then explaining how an ark might solve that problem. Putting forward a range of possible solutions helps signal your willingness to take responsibility for helping address the issue. You have not simply dumped the problem in someone else's lap. In so doing, you may reduce the defensiveness of the other party and minimize the likelihood of interpersonal conflict. Finally, close your assertive statement with an attempt to secure agreement from the other party. One might ask, "Do you concur with my assessment?" That question puts the onus on the other party to respond to your statement of concern.

Speaking up requires more than crafting the right series of statements, though. In large, complex organizations, individuals must pay close attention to social and political dynamics. They need to find a way to gain access to key decision-makers and to build support for their viewpoints. To begin, individuals must know their audience. Who are you trying to persuade? How do they think and make choices? What constitutes evidence to them? Some decision-makers rely heavily on data and formal analysis. Others depend on their intuition a great deal. Emotions play a major role for some decision-makers, but less so for others. When speaking up about a potential problem, individuals must understand these distinctions. If a key decision-maker proves highly analytical, you should not simply argue that your "gut" tells you that a problem exists. Marshaling data and conducting methodical analysis will prove more convincing. Individuals also must understand the historical background of the key decision-makers. Is this project "their baby"? Will they feel threatened if you argue that a problem exists? If so, individuals must take great care to avoid placing blame. Focus on the solution, and take ownership for helping resolve the issue.

Sometimes individuals cannot expect to persuade others that a problem exists on their own. They need help. Seeking allies and building coalitions are effective strategies in many situations. Individuals must remember that strength resides in numbers, particularly when one holds a dissenting view. A group may marginalize or dismiss the concerns of a lone voice trying to challenge the majority's perspective. However, if two or more people chime in together, the majority may find it much more difficult to dismiss these concerns with ease.[25]

When trying to present unwelcome news or a dissenting viewpoint, it helps to know who has influence with the senior executive you want to persuade. Most leaders rely on a trusted confidante at times for counsel and advice. That confidante serves as a useful sounding board.[26] He or she has the senior executive's ear. Others may serve as key gatekeepers who manage the flow of information to a senior leader. If an individual wants to be heard, particularly when bringing forth bad news, he or she must determine who these confidantes and gatekeepers are. One must attempt to bring these individuals onboard so that they can help make the case that a problem truly exists.

When speaking up as a dissenting voice, individuals must remember that their goal need not be to change people's minds immediately. Simply expressing an alternative perspective often causes others to think differently about a particular situation. Psychologists Charlan Nemeth and Julianne Kwan have shown that "Exposure to persistent minority views causes subjects to reexamine the issue and to engage in more divergent and original thought."[27] In an interesting experiment, they exposed individuals to a series of blue-colored slides, while a confederate purposefully judged these blue slides to be green. Then the researchers told the subjects about the results of prior studies (the results were concocted for purposes of the experiment). They informed some subjects that the confederate's judgment represented the majority viewpoint in earlier studies, and they told the others that the confederate's judgment represented the minority viewpoint in prior research. The researchers wanted to establish a perception on the part of the subjects that they were opposed by either a majority or a minority. After showing the colored slides, they asked all subjects to provide a series of word associations in response to the words "blue" and "green." Amazingly, the subjects who were made to believe that the confederate's judgment represented the minority viewpoint actually produced a higher quantity of word associations. *Moreover, those associations were more original!* Nemeth and Kwan found that opposition from a majority leads to more conventional thought. However, they concluded, "It is opposition by a *minority* that encourages originality, the use of varied strategies, and results in the detection of both more solutions and more novel solutions."[28] Amazingly, the researchers demonstrated that exposure to a minority view on a particular topic can stimulate originality on a *subsequent, related task*.

Other studies have confirmed these findings. When someone offers a dissenting view, it may not change the minds of the majority immediately. However, it tends to stimulate more divergent thinking. That creative thought may help others ultimately agree that a problem exists with the current course of action. When people come to that conclusion for themselves, they take ownership of the situation and commit to resolving the problem.[29] Table 7.1 summarizes the strategies that individuals can employ to speak up more effectively.

TABLE 7.1   How to Speak Up More Effectively

Strategy	Description
Know your audience	Learn about the person you are trying to persuade. Present your arguments in a way that fits that person's preferred mode of processing information.
Understand the history	Determine who will feel most threatened by your attempts to shine a spotlight on a particular problem. Avoid placing blame on that person; focus on how to improve the situation.
Seek allies and build coalitions	Strength resides in numbers. Find others who will support your viewpoint. Present a united front.
Work through key confidants and gatekeepers	Identify the individuals who have the ear of the person you ultimately must persuade. Seek them out, and try to bring them onboard first.
Focus first on divergent thinking	Remember that your near-term goal should not be to persuade everyone to adopt your view immediately. Begin by simply trying to encourage people to think differently about the situation at hand.
Present alternative solutions	Do not just point out the problem; offer a series of possible solutions. Make it clear that you want to help fix the problem.

Listening

Winston Churchill, one of history's greatest orators, once said, "Courage is what it takes to stand up and speak; courage is also what it takes to sit down and listen." When people come forward with problems and bad news, it helps if others listen genuinely and effectively to their concerns. Good listening must be active; you must interact with the speaker through questions, statements, and nonverbal cues. You must show them that you care about what they are saying and that you want to understand them more clearly.

Good listening begins with engagement. When students sit passively in a classroom, they act like empty vessels, hoping that the professor will fill them with knowledge. Much more learning takes place when professor and student engage interactively. Good listeners ask clarifying questions. They paraphrase what they have heard and play it back to test for understanding. They take notes, using both words and pictures/diagrams to record and synthesize what they have heard. Good listeners let a speaker know when they are confused, or when they need more information on a particular point.

Listeners must exercise a good deal of restraint, though. They have to refrain from jumping to conclusions based on a few early statements made by the speaker. That initial judgment may cause them to dismiss much of the rest of what the speaker has to say. Ralph Nichols describes how he encourages students to listen more effectively:

> "Listening efficiency drops to zero when the listeners react so strongly to one part of the presentation that they miss what follows. At the University of Minnesota we think this bad habit is so critical that, in the classes where we teach listening, we put at the top of every blackboard the words: Withhold evaluation until comprehension is complete—hear the speaker out. It is important that we understand the speaker's point of view fully before we accept or reject it."[30]

Distractions prove a major problem for many listeners. Turn off the phone and ignore the email for a few moments. Give the speaker your undivided attention. Avoiding distractions not only improves understanding, it also is the courteous thing to do. As someone speaks to you, make eye contact. Use gestures and body language to show that you are processing and reacting to what you have heard.

Nichols points out that people think faster than they speak. People speak one hundred to one hundred twenty-five words per minute, but they can think at four to five times that rate. The most effective listeners take advantage of that difference. They do not allow themselves to daydream. Instead, they begin to process what they have heard. They summarize it occasionally for themselves, and they try to identify the major themes being presented. They synthesize multiple ideas and seek connections among various points that have been made. They even try to anticipate what the speaker will say next. This active thought process helps ideas sink in deeply, and it improves recall in the future.

Finally, the best listeners do not spend a great deal of time worrying about how they will respond when the speaker is done. Poor listeners are obsessed with rehearsing what they will say when the other party stops talking. At times, the speaker may be only a short way through his or her statement, and the so-called listener already has decided how to respond. In business school case study discussions, the most frustrating episodes occur when a student puts forth a rehearsed comment she has prepared *prior to arriving at class.* She jumps into her dialogue and then wonders why the others seem dismayed by her comment, which does not fit into the flow of the discussion.

Train Teams, Not Individuals

In a recent special feature on leadership development, *Fortune* magazine focused on the best practices of companies known for building the capabilities of their people. Senior editor Geoffrey Colvin writes that the best companies for building leaders "develop teams, not just individuals." He quotes Jeffrey Immelt, CEO of General Electric:

> "'At the GE I grew up in, most of my training was individually based,' says Immelt. That led to problems. He'd attend a three-week program at Crotonville, but back at work 'I could use only 60% of what I'd learned because I needed others—my boss, my IT guy—to help with the rest.' And maybe they weren't onboard. Now GE takes whole teams and puts them through Crotonville together, where they make real decisions about their business. Result: 'There's no excuse for not doing it.'"[31]

Many organizations do train their people to communicate more effectively. They bring together individuals from various parts of the organization, and they try to develop their capabilities. Often, this training takes place in a leadership development program, perhaps for individuals who have been designated as "high potentials." However, many organizations make a crucial mistake as they design these developmental opportunities. They fail to occasionally bring together intact organizational teams to learn how members can communicate more effectively with one another. Some training can be done at the individual level, but the development of interpersonal communication capabilities often works best within a working group. Then the entire team can reflect on their past experiences, learn about ideas and concepts together, and practice new techniques with one another. That practice can take place in a safe setting with facilitators who can offer rapid and constructive feedback. The team then can put the new techniques to work when they have key issues to address back on the job.

As a leader, you must take responsibility for honing your own communication skills and for developing your people's capabilities. Surely you will hear from skeptics who doubt the efficacy of communication training. When the naysayers emerge, remind them of the Tenerife tragedy. Recount to them how aviation experts developed Crew Resource Management (CRM) techniques. Tell them how industry after industry has reported marked safety improvements thanks to CRM practices. Finally, remind them of Captain Al Haynes, who believes that CRM saved many lives on that day in Sioux City, Iowa, when he and his crew executed a remarkable crash landing of United Flight 232. As Haynes said, "If I hadn't used CRM...it's a cinch we wouldn't have made it."[32]

Endnotes

[1] This account of the Tenerife disaster draws on several sources: See Weick, K. (1990). "The vulnerable system: An analysis of the Tenerife air disaster." *Journal of Management*. 16(3): 571–593; Job, M. (1994). *Air Disaster: Volume 1*. Fyshwick, Australia: Aerospace Publications. In addition, see the following website for information: http://www.super70s.com/Super70s/Tech/Aviation/Disasters/77-03-27(Tenerife).asp.

[2] All the quotes in this section come from the original transcripts of the cockpit voice recorders. See the following website for the transcripts: http://www.pan-american.de/Desasters/Teneriff2.html.

[3] Weick, K. (1990). p. 582.

[4] Ibid.

[5] Ibid.

[6] Weiner, E. L., B. G. Kanki, and Robert L. Helmreich. (1995). *Cockpit Resource Management*. London: Academic Press.

[7] Flin, R., P. O'Connor, and K. Mearns. (2002). "Crew resource management: Improving team work in high reliability industries." *Team Performance Management*. 8:(3/4): 68–78.

[8] Helmreich, R. and H. C. Foushee. (1995). "Why crew resource management? Empirical and theoretical bases of human factors training in aviation." In R. Flin, P. O'Connor, and K. Mearns (eds.). *Cockpit Resource Management*. (3–45). London: Academic Press. The quote can be found on page 4.

[9] Ginnett, R. (1995). "Crews as groups: Their formation and their leadership." In R. Flin, P. O'Connor, and K. Mearns (eds.). *Cockpit Resource Management*. (71–98). London: Academic Press. This quote can be found on page 82.

[10] Ginnett, R. (1995). This quote can be found on page 90.

[11] http://yarchive.net/air/airliners/dc10_sioux_city.html.

[12] *Crew resource management: A positive change for the fire service*. (2003). International Association of Fire Chiefs. Fairfax, Virginia.

[13] During my time in graduate school, I taught Economics 10, the introductory micro- and macroeconomics course at Harvard College. The course head was Professor

Martin Feldstein, the distinguished economics professor and former Chairman of the Council of Economic Advisers in President Ronald Reagan's administration. Each year, he brought together the new graduate student teaching fellows for a weekend of training. I attended the first year as a trainee and in subsequent years as a trainer. Professor Feldstein always shared these words with incoming teachers.

[14] *Crew resource management: A positive change for the fire service*. (2003). International Association of Fire Chiefs. Fairfax, Virginia.

[15] Interview with Kelly Ison. He is a former U.S. Airways pilot. At the time of the interview in late 2006, Ison served as the President of Europe for Tomcat Global.

[16] The following information comes from the interview with Ison as well as from Airbus's booklet on flight operations briefings, which can be found at the following URL: http://www.airbus.com/store/mm_repository/safety_library_items/att00011205/media_object_file_FLT_OPS-CAB_OPS-SEQ01.pdf.

[17] Murphy, J. (2005). *Flawless Execution*. New York: Harper Collins. p. 93.

[18] Ibid, p. 95.

[19] David Breashears first mentioned this to me over lunch when I was working on my case study of the 1996 Mount Everest tragedy in 2002. Breashears and I have spoken numerous times over the past six years, and he has been kind enough to visit my classes several times. He has shared some keen insights into leadership based on his experience as an accomplished mountaineer and filmmaker.

[20] Hackman, R. (2002). *Leading Teams: Setting the Stage for Great Performances*. Boston: Harvard Business School Press.

[21] Powell, S. and R. Hill. (2006). "My copilot is a nurse: Using crew resource management in the OR." *AORN Journal*. 83(1): 178–206.

[22] My daughter Celia had a series of skin graft surgeries in 2006–2007 to address a large nevus on her ankle. Dr. Richard Bartlett performed the surgeries, and he did a remarkable job. These observations come from my time at the hospital.

[23] http://www.airbus.com/store/mm_repository/safety_library_items/att00011205/media_object_file_FLT_OPS-CAB_OPS-SEQ01.pdf; Powell, S. and R. Hill. (2006).

[24] *Crew Resource Management: A Positive Change for the Fire Service*. (2003). International Association of Fire Chiefs. Fairfax, Virginia.

[25] Many people believe that political behavior is detrimental in organizations. However, as Joseph Bower once wrote, "Politics is not pathology. It is a fact of large organization." Bower, J. (1970). *Managing the Resource Allocation Process*. Boston: Harvard Business School Division of Research. p. 305. Kathleen Eisenhardt and L. Jay Bourgeois found that political behavior—defined in terms of activities such as withholding information and behind-the-scenes coalition formation—leads to less effective decisions and poorer organizational performance. See Eisenhardt, K. and L. J. Bourgeois. (1988). "The politics of strategic decision making in high-velocity environments: Toward a midrange theory." *Academy of Management Journal*. 31(4): 737–770. However, other studies show that certain forms of political behavior can enhance organizational performance. For instance, Kanter, Sapolsky, Pettigrew, and

Pfeffer each have conducted studies that show that political activity such as coalition-building can prove helpful in building commitment and securing support for organizational decisions. See Kanter, R. (1983). *Change Masters*. New York: Simon and Schuster; Sapolsky, H. (1972). *The Polaris System Development: Bureaucratic and Programmatic Success in Government*. Cambridge: Harvard University Press; Pettigrew, A. (1973). *The Politics of Organizational Decision Making*. London: Tavistock; Pfeffer, J. (1992). *Managing with Power*. Boston: Harvard Business School Press. Why the discrepancy in these studies? It appears that the results depend on precisely how scholars define politics, as well as precisely how managers employ political tactics in organizations.

[26] Eisenhardt, K. M. (1989). "Making fast strategic decisions in high-velocity environments." *Academy of Management Journal*. 12: 543–576.

[27] Nemeth, C. and J. Kwan. (1985). "Originality of Word Associations as a Function of Majority vs. Minority Influence." *Social Psychology Quarterly*. 48(3): 277–282. This quote is from page 277.

[28] Ibid, p. 282.

[29] Charlan Nemeth has conducted a whole series of studies on this subject. For more information on this stream of research, see Nemeth, C. J. (2002). "Minority dissent and its 'hidden' benefits." *New Review of Social Psychology*. 2: 21–2.

[30] Nichols, R. (1960). "What can be done about listening." *The Supervisor's Notebook*. 22(1). For a copy of this article, see the following URL: http://www.dartmouth.edu/~acskills/docs/10_bad_listening_habits.doc.

[31] Colvin, G. "How top companies breed stars." *Fortune*. September 20, 2007.

[32] http://yarchive.net/air/airliners/dc10_sioux_city.html.

8

Watch the Game Film

"Look in the mirror, and don't be tempted to equate transient domination with either intrinsic superiority or prospects for extended survival."

—Stephen Jay Gould

The Pro Football Hall of Fame inducted Raymond Berry on July 28, 1973. That moment capped a remarkable career in which he had caught a record six hundred thirty-one passes. He teamed with quarterback Johnny Unitas to form one of the great quarterback-receiver tandems in football history. Together, they led the Baltimore Colts to two National Football League (NFL) championships.[1]

Berry's story is remarkable because of the rather unexceptional start to his career.[2] In high school, he played for a team coached by his father, yet he did not become a starter until his senior year. He was a skinny kid who lacked dazzling speed. He suffered from near-sightedness and a bad back. Berry wore special shoes because one of his legs was longer than the other. At Southern Methodist University, he caught a total of thirty-three passes in his entire career. The Baltimore Colts chose him in the twentieth round of the 1954 NFL draft; no other team expressed interest.

In Berry's first pro season, he caught only thirteen passes. The team did not fare much better, finishing in fourth place in its division. The offense ranked next to last in the league. Berry worked relentlessly, though, to improve his game. He watched countless hours of film, dissecting how the best receivers in the game excelled at their craft. He studied the Colts' opponents in great detail, trying to detect their tendencies and vulnerabilities on film. Today, all NFL coaches and players study film endlessly, but at the time, Berry was an exception. Teammates found his methods rather bizarre. Berry developed a wide array of maneuvers for getting open against defenses despite his limited speed—eighty-eight different moves by his estimation. Then, he practiced these moves relentlessly. He would simulate an entire game by himself during the off-season, trying to run each pattern "within inches of how they were diagrammed."[3]

Johnny Unitas joined the Baltimore Colts at the start of Berry's second season, having been cut by the Pittsburgh Steelers the previous year. Unitas hoped to catch on as a backup quarterback. Soon, Unitas and Berry formed a bond—two eager young players desperate to improve, make the team, and contribute in a meaningful way. In the evenings, Berry asked Unitas to study film with him in his apartment. The two men stayed on the field after regular team practice for hours, working on each pass pattern repeatedly. Berry named each type of catch. He wanted to run perfect patterns, and he practiced making the most challenging catches repeatedly. Berry once described the importance of these practices to one of his teammates: "He (Unitas) has to know that after three and two-tenths seconds, this is where you are going to be. You've got to time it up with him. It's like music. The same beat has to be playing in all of our heads."[4]

The two players soon became starters for the Colts. In 1958, Unitas led the league in passing touchdowns, and Berry topped the NFL in receptions.[5] In that same year, Unitas and Berry led the Colts to the NFL championship against the New York Giants. On December 28, 1958 in Yankee Stadium, the Giants led the Colts 17–14 with two minutes and twenty seconds remaining in the contest. The Colts offense had the ball at their own fourteen-yard line, far from where they needed to be to attempt a game-tying field goal. After more than a minute of trying to attack the Giants' defense, the Colts had made little progress. With just seventy-five seconds remaining, they stood at the twenty-five yard line. Time was running out.

Unitas hoped to throw to Berry along the sidelines on the next play, according to Mark Bowden, who wrote a wonderful book about this historic championship contest.[6] However, Giants defensive coach Tom Landry anticipated the play. Just before Unitas took the snap, a Giants linebacker shifted out to line up near Berry, as instructed by Landry. Now, Berry faced two defenders, typically meaning that a pass play to him would not succeed. Berry had not seen such a defensive maneuver by the Giants when he studied film of their previous games. However, in that moment, he recalled a film session with Unitas several years earlier, in which the two men had noticed this defensive strategy employed by a different opponent. Berry and Unitas had detected a problem with this defensive scheme, and they concocted a way to capitalize on this weakness.

Now the two men had an opportunity to employ their counter-strategy, but they could not speak with one another. They stood many yards apart, with the play about to begin. Berry simply gazed in Unitas's direction, hoping that they were on the same page. As the ball was snapped, Berry did not run the pattern that Unitas had called for in the huddle. Instead, he ran a different pattern, the one they had devised several years earlier in his apartment. As Berry made his move, Unitas anticipated precisely what his receiver would do in that situation. Unitas connected with Berry on a pass play that covered twenty-five yards. It was like music, the same beat playing in both men's minds. Several plays later, the Colts had tied the game. Ultimately, they prevailed in overtime in a game many still consider the greatest ever played. Berry finished the contest with a then-record twelve catches for one hundred seventy-eight yards and a touchdown. The skinny kid who barely made the team a few years earlier had become a record-breaking champion.[7]

Athletes not only study film on the competition; they watch themselves perform too. They study film of their own performances to identify problems and flaws. Baseball player Tony Gwynn became a pioneer in the use of video in his sport. When Gwynn joined the San Diego Padres in 1982, all football teams had adopted Berry's film-study methods, but baseball players had not. In his second season, Gwynn fell into a miserable slump, partly due to a wrist injury suffered during the winter. Gwynn purchased a video cassette recorder for $500, and his wife Alicia began videotaping each of his at-bats. He reviewed the tapes and identified the flaws in his hitting approach. Gwynn said, "I came back from a trip and looked at the tapes and I knew immediately what was wrong. From that point on, I hit like .350 and had a 25-game hitting streak."[8] He never finished a season in his long and storied career with a batting average lower than the one he compiled in that season (which was still a very good .309).[9]

Gwynn became a fanatic about using video to study his swing, as well as the pitchers whom he opposed. He carried videos with him wherever he traveled. Teammates nicknamed him "Captain Video." At first, they viewed his near-obsession with video as rather odd, much like Berry's teammates had. Over time, his peers became believers. After reviewing the video, Gwynn practiced with intensity. Baseball coach Dave Engle once said, "You could take the next five guys who put the most time in, and added together, they would not put as much time in as Tony."[10] He did not just try to hit the ball during batting practice; he imagined a particular situation and practiced the precise swing he would use in that circumstance. Alternatively, Gwynn might focus on correcting a mechanical flaw that he noticed on video; he would practice that particular refinement over and over. During practice, he focused as much, if not more, on the process of hitting as on the outcome of each swing.

In 1984, Gwynn's first full season using video, he won the batting title (for highest batting average in the National League). By the end of his career, he had earned that honor eight times, tying the National League record.[11] He entered the Hall of Fame on July 29, 2007 as one of the greatest pure hitters in the history of baseball.[12] His peers recognized him as one of the most astute students of hitting that the game had ever seen.

The story of these two athletes demonstrates two important lessons regarding how effective problem-finding can lead to superior performance. First, we see the value of "watching the game film." Like Berry and Gwynn, companies should study their past performance, as well as their rivals' performance. They should search for problems and vulnerabilities that can be exploited. Of course, many companies do engage in benchmarking and competitor intelligence. They also conduct "after-action reviews" to identify problems experienced during a major project or initiative. However, the promise of these learning activities often remains unrealized. Firms encounter a series of common pitfalls that make these activities far less productive than they can be. In this chapter, we will take a look at these pitfalls and identify ways in which leaders can avoid them.

Second, we learn from these two athletes' stories that elite performers do not excel simply due to innate talent. They hone their skills through a great deal of practice. In fact, research shows that individuals in many different fields achieve greatness through hard work, not simply raw talent. However, research shows that it takes a particular type of preparation to truly excel; scholars have described it as "deliberate practice." Berry and Gwynn adopted this approach to preparation and skill refinement. Through their practice regimens, Berry and Gwynn discovered the small problems and flaws that prevented them from achieving their potential. Some individuals work very hard, but they adopt the wrong practice techniques. Research demonstrates that elite performers engage in an immense amount of highly effective "deliberate practice" over their careers. This chapter explains deliberate practice and describes how it facilitates effective problem-finding. Moreover, we will explain why many firms do not provide employees with sufficient opportunities for deliberate practice, or why they encourage the wrong types of training and preparation. We also will take a look at how some companies have provided effective practice opportunities for their employees.

After-Action Reviews: Promise and Peril

Many companies have tried to conduct lessons-learned exercises after the completion of major projects. Outside of sports, the U.S. Army became one of the first large organizations to develop a systematic approach to postmortem analysis. The Army developed its after-action review (AAR) procedure in the 1970s, although widespread adoption did not take place for a number of years. Each reflection-and-review process focuses on four fundamental questions:

- What did we set out to do?
- What actually happened?
- Why did it happen?
- What will we do next time?[13]

Harvard Professor David Garvin has conducted extensive research on the Army's use of AARs. He reports that the Army now conducts these lessons-learned exercises routinely. The Army has learned that these reviews must become "a state of mind where everybody is continuously assessing themselves, their units, and their organizations and asking how they can improve."[14] AARs must be conducted immediately after a mission has been completed so that the key events can be recalled easily and accurately by all participants. Garvin points out that the process requires skilled facilitators and a willingness on the part of military leaders not to dominate the discussions, even to admit their own mistakes. Finally, the Army works very hard to create a climate of openness and candor, and facilitators actively discourage finger-pointing and the assignment of blame during these reviews.[15]

Other organizations have adopted the Army's techniques. For instance, many hospitals try to conduct lessons-learned exercises after medical accidents. The Joint Commission on Accreditation of Health-care Organizations (JCAHO) now requires hospitals to conduct thorough reviews following serious medical accidents, which health care professionals describe as sentinel events. Many hospitals also have expanded the use of such reviews to less serious incidents, going well beyond the mandate of the accreditation body. For instance, at Children's Hospital in Minneapolis, the Patient Safety Steering Committee chose to conduct "focused event studies" after a wide range of less serious incidents, as well as "near misses"—instances in which an accident was narrowly averted and no harm came to a patient.[16] Dr. Chris Robison, Associate Director of Medical Affairs, serves as one of the facilitators of this review process. Like the Army, Children's focuses on establishing clear ground rules for how these reviews should be conducted, and it follows a structured procedure for analyzing each incident. Here's how Robison kicked off the review of a morphine overdose incident that took place at the hospital:

> "We have several objectives today: to understand what happened, to identify opportunities for improvement, and to support the caregivers, patient, and family that were involved. Today, we will focus primarily on documenting the process flow of yesterday's events. We have three ground rules for this discussion. First, it is a blameless environment; we are not here to find a scapegoat but to identify failures in our operating system. We want to reveal all of the issues and problems in an open discussion. Second, this process is confidential. Please do not reveal the name of the patient or the identity of the caregivers. Third, we ask you to think creatively about how to improve our systems and processes. Try to envision the patient as your own child and to identify systems that you would like to have in place to ensure your child's safety."[17]

During the session, Robison asked questions in order to identify, understand, and diagram the sequence of events that led to the morphine overdose. As people spoke, Robison recorded the details carefully on a whiteboard. He found that creating a visual aid, such as a process flow diagram documenting the sequence of events, helped facilitate a constructive, fact-based discussion. Robison tried to ensure that the physicians did not dominate. He frequently asked, "Have we documented the process accurately? Are we missing something?" Ultimately, the group agreed on the detailed sequence of events that had taken place, and from there, it identified a number of opportunities for improvement.[18]

While some organizations have employed AARs quite effectively, most firms struggle to capture the true value of such lessons-learned exercises. Attempts to review projects become blame games in some companies. In others, the procedure becomes slow, cumbersome, and bureaucratic. The review process drags out far too long; in some cases, it does not even begin until well after the project has been completed. At that point, memories of key events have become foggy, and hindsight biases cloud people's perspectives. Individuals write lengthy reports on the lessons learned from a project, and the binders collect dust on someone's bookshelf. Little follow-up occurs to ensure that improvement ideas are implemented. As noted organizational learning expert Peter Senge has said, "The Army's After Action Review is arguably one of the most successful organizational learning methods yet devised. Yet, most every corporate effort to graft this truly innovative practice into their culture has failed because, again and again, people reduce the living practice of AARs to a sterile technique."[19]

Why do many AAR processes fail? Many firms stumble for the reasons just cited: the inability to create a climate of candor, a lack of skilled facilitators, and a poor follow-up process for ensuring that improvement ideas are implemented efficiently. The problems extend beyond those usual suspects, though. First, many organizations study past projects in a compartmentalized fashion. A small group of people come together, but they do not necessarily understand the entire picture. For instance, at one firm in my research, a group of marketing managers came together to study a failed product launch. However, they did not involve key individuals from other organizational units, including operations, logistics, and procurement. This small group did not understand the entire system of activities involved in the product launch. The individuals involved in the postmortem analysis did not understand the interconnections among the activities of people in multiple functions. They missed the fact that some problems occurred during the handoffs that took place from one unit to another. Individuals found themselves jumping to conclusions about the mistakes that had occurred without understanding all the facts.

Dr. Robison has learned that assembling the right group of people, from diverse units of the organization, is essential to the success of an after-action review. People need to develop a systemic perspective about failures. Moreover, you need to come to a clear understanding of the facts before trying to ascertain cause-and-effect relationships. He explains:

> "I don't think we could have gotten as thorough an understanding of what happened to Matthew if I had talked with people individually. There was so much point and counterpoint during the meeting. We saw the event from the nurse's perspective and then from the respiratory therapist's perspective and then the doctor's. It is not that people only perceive things consistent with their viewpoint, but that they have actually only touched one part of the elephant. I have found that most people think that they know where the failure was and what failed. However, when they come into one of these meetings, they realize that there were ten possible defenses in the system. They come to understand its complexity. They recognize that there were aspects of the situation they didn't even know existed. These focused event analyses develop disciples that then go out into the organization understanding the complexity of medical accidents."[20]

After-action reviews also fail because people do not have an accurate recollection of what happened, and they haven't kept a complete record of the key events that took place during a particular project or initiative. When possible, the Army compiles extensive audio and videotapes during its training exercises, as well as during some actual missions, so as to have an objective record of activities to examine during the review process. The Army obtains data from instrumentation technology, and it employs observers who record key events.[21] In essence, it compiles a "game film" much like a coach or athlete does in sports. In so doing, the Army does not rely only on individuals' recollections, which may be incomplete or biased. The videotape never lies, as many coaches say.

Hospitals have the patients' medical charts that they can review, as well as the results of various tests and procedures. These archival documents provide objective evidence that helps individuals compile an accurate picture of what occurred. During the *Columbia* space shuttle's final mission, NASA taped key Mission Management Team meetings, and it stored emails and other key documents. That record of events enabled the Columbia Accident Investigation Board to piece together precisely what had transpired during the mission as it tried to determine the causes of the tragedy.[22] Airlines, of course, have flight data and voice recorders on every plane. Most companies cannot videotape activities and events, but they can consider what evidence will be needed to conduct an effective after-action review *as they launch a major project*. In so doing, firms can plot their data-collection strategy. Managers can encourage employees to store key documents, record minutes after crucial meetings, and track key metrics and milestones as a project is planned and executed. Everyone involved in a project should be asking: What evidence should I be collecting that will enable us to perform a useful after-action review in the future?[23]

Many firms only conduct postmortems—they study failures, but not successes. However, many small problems and mistakes occur even during the most successful projects. If these issues are not addressed, they may escalate and contribute to a major failure in the future. Moreover, many companies examine projects in isolation. They fail to compare and contrast a particular initiative with other projects either inside or outside the organization. Comparison helps protect against spurious conclusions. When we study a single project, it becomes rather easy to jump to conclusions about what factors contributed to that outcome. However, we may not have identified the correct cause-and-effect relationship; we attribute the outcome to the wrong factors. Examining how the same behaviors and activities played out in multiple situations, perhaps some more successful than others, enables us to refine our attributions and conclusions. We develop much richer models of cause and effect.

Research supports this contention that after-action reviews should invoke comparisons among multiple projects, and that enterprises should not only study failures. Tel Aviv University scholars Schmuel Ellis and Inbar Davidi examined after-event reviews conducted by Israeli military forces. They compared soldiers who conducted post-event reflection exercises after successful and unsuccessful navigation exercises with soldiers who reviewed only failures. Ellis and Davidi discovered that "contemplation of successful events stimulated the learners to generate more hypotheses about their performance."[24] The soldiers who systematically analyzed both successes and failures developed richer mental models of cause and effect. Perhaps most importantly, these soldiers *performed better on subsequent missions.*[25]

After-action reviews fail to achieve promised results for one final reason. Organizations often do not identify near-miss incidents and review them systematically. Near misses occur in all sorts of enterprises, and they represent powerful opportunities for learning and reflection. However, many individuals simply breathe a sigh of relief when a near miss occurs. They do not surface the issue for discussion and evaluation. The results can be disastrous. In April 1994, two U.S. fighter jets mistakenly shot down two American Black Hawk helicopters on a humanitarian mission in Northern Iraq's no-fly zone. As it turned out, a near miss had occurred a short time before this tragic incident. The near miss never surfaced at higher levels of the organization; officers did not have an opportunity to analyze it closely. If they had, a tragedy may have been averted.[26]

Scholars James March, Lee Sproull, and Michael Tamuz have argued for the value of studying near-misses quite closely. They pointed out that, "Organizations learn from experience, but learning seems problematic when history offers only meager samples of experience."[27] For instance, an airline rarely experiences a fatal aviation accident. It becomes difficult to learn from experience if the sample size proves so limited. Moreover, we have a tendency to "overgeneralize" the lessons from a single, yet quite memorable, episode in an organization's history. Near-misses protect us against this type of flawed learning; they provide an opportunity to increase the sample size from which we can derive lessons. With respect to the field of aviation, these scholars explained that, "Information on near-accidents augments the relatively sparse history of real accidents and has been used to redesign aircraft, air traffic control systems, airports, cockpit routines, and pilot training procedures."[28]

At Children's Hospital, nurses initiated "good-catch logs" to document near misses and trigger further analysis. Good-catch logs are located in locked medication rooms on each floor of the hospital. If nurses "catch" a problem that could have resulted in an accident, they describe the situation in the log. Nurses felt comfortable with this process because they could record events anonymously. As one staff member noted, "Here, nurses can report accidents waiting to happen."[29] Good-catch logs are a perfect example of proactive problem-finding. Teams in each unit periodically reviewed the logs and then initiated process improvements based on an analysis of these near-miss incidents. As nurses realized that their entries often led to concrete changes, they became more comfortable with writing in the logs. One nurse explained, "Now we feel like someone is listening and doing things about our concerns."[30] Every organization should strive to create its own version of this hospital's good-catch log if it wants to discover problems proactively and improve its learning processes.

Competitor Intelligence: Promise and Peril

Like the star athletes Raymond Berry and Tony Gwynn, companies need to study the competition as well. They have to compile a game film that can be dissected and analyzed. Such evaluation enables us to spot our own problems as well as the weaknesses and vulnerabilities of our rivals. Many firms engage in competitor intelligence and benchmarking. However, these activities do not always prove as useful as leaders expect. Competitive-intelligence expert Leonard Fuld explains:

> "Sometimes, people just get in the way of valid intelligence because their minds block out reality. There is a great psychological component to analyzing and convincing others of critical intelligence. For too many managers, denial, rationalization, groupthink, or not-invented-here attitudes are among the reasons why a competitive revelation never bubbles to the surface."[31]

Let's take a closer look at how and why many attempts to analyze our competitors do not bear fruit. First, many firms engage in highly generic analysis. They conduct SWOT analysis (strengths, weaknesses, opportunities, and threats), but that exercise leaves them with a laundry list rather than a clear understanding of what issues matter most.[32] They also define capabilities and vulnerabilities too broadly. For instance, a firm might categorize a rival as having a stronger supply chain management capability. However, it does not dig deeper to understand whether its competitor's advantage lies in procurement, inbound logistics, outbound logistics, inventory management, and so on. To be more precise, companies ought to consider compiling a precise record of how a rival conducts a particular project or initiative. For instance, an effective competitor analysis might track a competitor's new product launch in great detail and then compare and contrast that effort with the firm's own recent launch. Such efforts give the analysis more precision and depth, and they provide opportunities for valuable direct comparisons.

Many firms involve a narrow set of employees in the competitive-intelligence process. They have an individual or small unit, often within the corporate strategic planning organization, responsible for gathering data about rivals. They do not take advantage of the fact that many frontline employees are learning about the competition on a daily basis. Effective firms tap into and synthesize that fragmented local knowledge. They involve frontline employees not only as data gatherers, but also as analysts who can help senior leaders derive conclusions from this data. The frontline employees often do not have the same blinders that may distort the judgments and conclusions of senior executives. Since senior executives have set the current strategy, they may not be as willing to admit where rivals have outmaneuvered them.

Benchmarking efforts frequently entail the creation of a mountain of quantitative data. The numbers compare and contrast organizations using a multitude of metrics. However, firms may become lost in the numbers and ignore crucial qualitative information about the competition. The numbers also may deceive us, since it proves difficult to make perfect apples-to-apples comparisons among firms' financial results. Leonard Fuld argues that overemphasizing the numbers creates a "one-dimensional blindness" in competitor intelligence. He advocates careful attention to "soft, qualitative information."[33] For instance, many airlines have tried to understand the secrets of Southwest Airlines' success. Without question, Southwest has made a number of strategic trade-offs that have enabled it to build a unique business model that cannot be easily imitated. However, the company's success hinges as much on its culture as on its hard assets and investments. As company founder Herb Kelleher has said, "What keeps me awake at night are the intangibles. It's the intangibles that are the hardest thing for a competitor to imitate, so my biggest fear is that we lose the esprit de corps, the culture, the spirit. If we ever do lose that, we'll have lost our most important competitive asset."[34]

Perhaps most importantly, we must remember to assess the leaders of our rival firms, rather than treating the organization as a monolithic black box. Who is making the decisions at the top, and what is their mindset? Do we understand their historical pattern of behavior vis-à-vis key rivals? Is the firm publicly held, or is it a privately held, family-owned enterprise? Such qualitative factors must be considered as we assess the competition. Think of a typical football coach. He does not simply assess the statistics of his opponents. He also wants to know how that rival behaved in a wide range of situations, including any prominent tendencies that the opposing coaches have exhibited throughout their careers. He uses the game film to look far beyond the numbers.

Finally, competitive-intelligence efforts falter because organizations adopt a narrow perspective. They focus too intently on their direct rivals. Companies often pay insufficient attention to potential new entrants, firms that offer substitute products, and suppliers or buyers who might forward- or backward-integrate. As an example, consider how Polaroid might have performed a competitor analysis in the early 1990s. In terms of instant cameras, Polaroid had a dominant position. After years of having a virtual monopoly in the U.S., Polaroid had watched Kodak enter the instant-camera market in the mid-1970s, but then exit in 1986. However, in terms of substitutes, Polaroid should have had many other firms on its radar screen. One-hour photo processing was becoming more widespread. Kodak had introduced one-time-use disposable cameras in 1987, and other firms had followed. Sales had become substantial by the early 1990s. Digital camera technology was emerging. With the emergence of digital technology, new electronics and computing firms, not previously in the camera business, stood poised to enter the market. In short, an effective competitor analysis would have entailed a wide-ranging look at potential rivals.[35]

The best firms do not stop there. They try to learn from firms well beyond their industry. They compare themselves against firms that will never become competitors, but that have a process or approach worth exploring. Consider how many product-design firms operate. When developing a new product, they do not simply study how other companies have designed that item. For instance, Pentagram, a California-based design firm, took an interesting approach to developing the high-end Fuego barbeque grill: They visited a luxury car dealer that sold Lamborghinis and Bentleys. They came up with ideas for how to fashion the grill's temperature gauge as well as how to add the look and feel of luxury to the grill. That out-of-the-box comparison enabled the designers to spot problems with more-traditional barbeque grills that detracted from their appearance and functionality.[36]

Deliberate Practice

Tony Gwynn and Raymond Berry not only watched a great deal of film on their opponents; they also spent an enormous amount of time practicing their craft. Sometimes, they began by working to resolve a problem they had already identified. On other occasions, focused repetitions helped them discover a problem that hindered their performance. Through practice, they developed a more refined mental model of the cause-and-effect relationships that drove their performance; they could spot the problems that led to failure much more easily.

K. Anders Ericsson and his colleagues have studied star performers in many fields, such as athletics, chess, and music.[37] He chose those fields because one can measure performance over time quite precisely. His research demonstrates that "important characteristics of experts' superior performance are acquired through experience and that the effect of practice on performance is larger than earlier believed possible."[38] Put another way, "experts are always made, not born."[39]

Ericsson documents how elite performers practice for an incredible amount of time during their lifetimes. For instance, one study examined three groups of violinists of differing abilities at the Music Academy of West Berlin. The best young violinists, as evaluated by the school instructors, accumulated an average of 7,410 hours of practice by age eighteen. That exceeded the next-best group by more than 2,000 hours and the least-talented set by 4,000 hours.[40]

The hours alone do not determine success, though. Elite performers do not simply exhibit extraordinary diligence and determination. They engage in what Ericsson calls "deliberate practice." *Fortune* magazine writer Geoffrey Colvin explains how a golfer such as Tiger Woods approaches practice far differently from those who hit the links a few weekends each summer:

> "Simply hitting a bucket of balls is not deliberate practice, which is why most golfers don't get better. Hitting an eight-iron three hundred times with a goal of leaving the ball within twenty feet of the pin eighty percent of the time, continually observing results and making appropriate adjustments, and doing that for hours each day—that's deliberate practice."[41]

When elite performers engage in deliberate practice, they set a specific performance improvement goal, and they engage in a task that provides immediate feedback. Moreover, deliberate practice involves focusing on the things that elite performers don't do well. Many of us tend to practice that at which we already excel in our leisure sport activities. Ericsson and his colleagues point out that "Research across domains shows that it is only by working at what you can't do that you turn into the expert you want to become."[42] Consider the example of basketball legend Larry Bird. When he entered the National Basketball Association, he did not have a strong left-handed shot. He worked on it relentlessly over the years. As it turned out, he made several of the most clutch shots of his career with his left hand in critical playoff games. In 1981, the Boston Celtics faced the Philadelphia 76ers in the final game of the Eastern Conference Championship Series. With the game tied and less than a minute left, Bird drained a difficult left-handed bank shot to give the Celtics a lead that they would not relinquish. The practice paid off handsomely.[43]

Deliberate practice consists of extensive repetition of the very same activity, so as to hone a particular skill. It emphasizes focus over variety in the building of skills—working on one thing at a time. As famous tennis instructor Vic Braden said, "Losers have tons of variety. Champions just take pride in learning to hit the same old boring winning shots." Finally, deliberate practice means paying close attention to your technique, not simply the results you achieve. As Braden argues, "You have to be process-oriented."[44]

Can business leaders engage in deliberate practice to improve their performance? Colvin concludes that "Many elements of business, in fact, are directly practicable. Presenting, negotiating, delivering evaluations, deciphering financial statements—you can practice them all."[45] Ericsson concurs. He points out that even the most accomplished leaders can practice skills such as persuasive communication. He notes, "Bear in mind that even Winston Churchill, one of the most charismatic figures of the twentieth century, practiced his oratory style in front of a mirror."[46]

Many companies fail to capitalize on opportunities to build deliberate practice into their employee-development programs. Far too many corporate universities continue to incorporate a substantial dose of passive learning into their programs. Passive learning consists of instruction in which the participant sits waiting for the teacher to impart wisdom. We certainly do not develop expertise in key managerial skills by listening to someone lecture us on a particular topic. We have to get our hands dirty and work on our skills to improve.

Some firms have embraced active-learning methods, such as simulations and experiential exercises. These employee-development techniques provide real opportunities for deliberate practice. Participants participate in a realistic scenario, attempt certain methods and techniques, and receive rapid constructive feedback. For years, airline pilots honed their skills through the use of complex, realistic simulations. Today, these simulation methodologies have begun to spread to a wide variety of industries and firms.

Video game technology has fueled growth in the development and use of realistic simulations that provide opportunities for deliberate practice. Consider the case of Hilton Garden Inn. In January 2008 the company launched Ultimate Team Play, an interactive training simulation for its hotel employees. The game puts staff members in a virtual hotel. Employees take on roles such as front desk, housekeeping, food and beverage, and maintenance personnel. They perform tasks such as answering the phone, checking guests in and out of their rooms, and the like. They encounter various scenarios and must respond to guest requests. The game produces a SALT (Satisfaction and Loyalty Tracking) score for the virtual hotel, based on how effectively the staff members perform during the simulation. The SALT metric represents the actual tool used to evaluate Hilton Garden Inn locations. Adrian Kurre, senior vice president at the company, explains the value of the SALT metric: "Including SALT was key because it really emphasizes to the entire team that no matter what role they have or what job they do, each person ultimately affects the guest's overall hotel experience."[47] By using this simulation, employees can work on key skills while receiving immediate feedback. They can repeat similar scenarios many times. Most importantly, they do not have to practice on actual customers; the virtual hotel provides a way for inexperienced personnel to improve without sacrificing the actual experience of Hilton Garden Inn guests.

UPS has adopted an even more far-reaching approach to creating opportunities for deliberate practice.[48] UPS encountered a problem several years ago, when young workers seemed to be taking longer to achieve proficiency in key skills. Many of them quit in their first few months at the company. These Generation Y employees did not seem to enjoy UPS's standard training methods. For years, UPS taught hundreds of rules and policies to its new drivers in a lengthy series of lectures. The company has since transformed its training practices to address the unique ways in which Generation Y workers tend to gather information, communicate, and learn. UPS shifted to an approach that emphasizes hands-on learning.

UPS opened its new $34 million 11,500-square-foot Integrad training center in Landover, Maryland in 2007. The facility consists of a series of hands-on learning tools. For instance, at one station, the company has placed a transparent UPS truck filled with packages. Instructors explain and then demonstrate how to load and unload a truck safely and efficiently. They show employees the company's incredibly precise rules and policies in action, rather than simply lecturing about them. Employees then have multiple opportunities to practice these tasks. Individuals identify problems that hinder their performance, and they try to correct these issues. At another station, UPS has created a slip-and-fall simulator. This rather fun exercise helps employees learn how to adjust their bodies as they begin to fall, so as to prevent serious injury. By reducing accident rates, UPS saves a great deal of money. Finally, the outdoor parking lot at this facility simulates a community, and trainees have an opportunity to drive a truck and serve customers. The town has model homes and stores, several street signs, and a UPS drop box. Employees drive through the town, and they practice conducting various tasks. Others play the role of customers in the town. As the employees practice, the instructors provide them rapid feedback on their performance. Over time, the instructors ratchet up the difficulty of the tasks. Although UPS adopted this approach with Generation Y employees in mind, the principles apply to people of all ages. We all benefit from hands-on learning opportunities. Active learning beats passive learning; deliberate practice enables people of all generations to improve and refine their skills.

Looking in the Mirror

Bill Parcells has achieved remarkable success as a professional football coach. He won two Super Bowls with the New York Giants, and he turned around several other losing franchises. With the New England Patriots, he inherited a team that won only two games and lost fourteen in the previous season. Several years later, Parcells took the team to the Super Bowl. With the New York Jets, he took over a team that had won only one contest the previous season. In two seasons, Parcells had the Jets competing in the conference championship game. Even with the Dallas Cowboys, where he enjoyed less success, he managed to take the team to the playoffs twice in four years. The franchise had won only five games in each of the three seasons prior to his arrival.[49]

Many people have noted that Parcells rarely seems happy about his team's performance regardless of whether they have won or lost. In fact, he often appears especially dour after a victory. His protégé, Bill Belichick, adopts a similar approach now as head coach of the New England Patriots—a team he has led to three Super Bowl championships. On many occasions, Belichick is critical of his team even when they win. He focuses on the team's mistakes as he dissects the game film. He drives them hard in practice, not letting them become complacent after a win. The two men both seem to find it hard to enjoy victory.

Parcells and Belichick offer a lesson for all leaders. We certainly do not propose that leaders should become miserable after their successes. However, they can take a hard look in the mirror after both success and failure. Leaders can watch the film, searching for the problems and mistakes, even when the outcome was highly successful. They can refine all the organization's critical learning and review processes. When many of us look in the mirror, particularly after a successful venture, we see a very positive image. Belichick and Parcells stare into the mirror, always looking for the warts. They search for problems consistently and relentlessly. All leaders need to help their organizations look in the mirror without being blinded by success. As noted evolutionary biologist Stephen Jay Gould once said, "Look in the mirror, and don't be tempted to equate transient domination with either intrinsic superiority or prospects for extended survival."

Endnotes

[1] http://www.profootballhof.com/hof/years.html.

[2] Mark Bowden has written a marvelous book about the 1958 NFL championship game between the Baltimore Colts and the New York Giants. He profiles Raymond Berry at length in that book. This account draws from his meticulous research. See Bowden, M. (2008). *The Best Game Ever: Giants vs. Colts, 1958, and the Birth of the Modern NFL*. New York: Atlantic Monthly Press.

[3] http://www.profootballhof.com/hof/member.jsp?player_id=25.

[4] Bowden. (2008). p. 68.

[5] http://www.pro-football-reference.com/.

[6] Bowden. (2008).

[7] Ibid.

[8] http://www.sportingnews.com/archives/gwynn/hit_masters_prep.html.

[9] http://www.baseball-reference.com/.

[10] Kepner, T. "Mets salute hitter who can't be beaten." *New York Times*. August 15, 2001.

[11] http://www.baseballlibrary.com/ballplayers/player.php?name=tony_gwynn_1960.

[12] Sandomir, R. "At Hall of Fame, Day Dedicated to Two Icons." *New York Times*. July 30, 2007.

[13] Garvin, D. (2000). *Learning in Action: A Guide to Putting the Learning Organization to Work*. Boston: Harvard Business School Press. p. 107.

[14] Garvin, D. (2000). p. 106.

[15] Garvin, D. (2000).

[16] Edmondson, A., M. Roberto, and A. Tucker. (2002). "Children's Hospital and Clinics (A)." Harvard Business School Case Study No. 9-302-050.

[17] Edmondson, A., M. Roberto, and A. Tucker. (2002). p. 2.

[18] Ibid.

[19] http://www.gojlc.com/articles/After-Action-Reviews-Ray-Jorgensen.pdf.

[20] Edmondson, A., M. Roberto, and A. Tucker. (2002). p. 10.

[21] Garvin, D. (2000).

[22] For more information on the *Columbia* shuttle accident, see the multimedia case study I developed with Professors Richard Bohmer and Amy Edmondson, our research associates Erika Ferlins and Laura Feldman, and an amazing technical team led by Melissa Dailey. Roberto, M., R. Bohmer, A. Edmondson, L. Feldman, and E. Ferlins. (2005). "Columbia's Final Mission, The." Harvard Business School Multi-Media Case Study No. 9-305-032. For a scholarly treatment of the disaster, see our book chapter: Edmondson, A., M. Roberto, R. Bohmer, L. Feldman, and E. Ferlins.

(2005). "The Recovery Window: Organizational Learning Following Ambiguous Threats in High-Risk Organizations." In M. Farjoun and W. Starbuck (eds.). *Organization at the Limit: Lessons from the Columbia Disaster*. London: Blackwell Publishers. For an article about the tragedy written for a managerial audience, see Roberto, M., R. Bohmer, and A. Edmondson. (2006). "Facing Ambiguous Threats." *Harvard Business Review*. November: 106–113.

[23] At times, firms may wish to break a large project down into smaller pieces to reduce risk, enhance flexibility, and maximize opportunities for learning. In the strategic management literature, scholars have described a concept called "real options." The notion is that a firm might choose not to embark on a major project in one giant leap. Instead, it may make a small investment with the option to proceed with the remainder of the project at some future date. In the period prior to "exercising the option," the firm can learn a great deal about the situation. The learning will help managers determine if and when to proceed. Moreover, an effective after-action review of the first phase can help improve the implementation of the remainder of the project. Firms, therefore, might wish to look for the "real options" embedded in major investment opportunities, and then utilize after-action reviews within these projects to help maximize the value of the options. For more on this concept, refer to the following two books: Dixit, A. and R. Pindyck. (1994). *Investment under Uncertainty*. Princeton, NJ: Princeton University Press; Trigeorgis, L. (1996). *Real Options: Managerial Flexibility and Strategy in Resource Allocation*. Cambridge, MA: MIT Press.

[24] Ellis, S. and I. Davidi. (2005). "After-event reviews: Drawing lessons from successful and failed experience." *Journal of Applied Psychology*. 90(5): 857–871. The quote is found on page 866.

[25] Ibid.

[26] Snook, S. (2000). *Friendly Fire: The Accidental Shootdown of U.S. Black Hawks Over Northern Iraq*. Princeton, NJ: Princeton University Press.

[27] March, J., L. Sproull, and M. Tamuz. (1991). "Learning from samples of one or fewer." *Organization Science*. 2(1): 1-13, p. 1.

[28] Ibid, p. 5.

[29] Edmondson, A., M. Roberto, and A. Tucker. (2002). p. 12.

[30] Ibid.

[31] Fuld, L. (2006). *The Secret Language of Competitive Intelligence*. New York: Crown Business.

[32] Kenneth Andrews was one of the pioneers in the field of strategic management who popularized the SWOT framework for strategy formulation. See Andrews, K. (1987). *The Concept of Corporate Strategy*. 3rd Edition. Homewood, IL: Irwin.

[33] Fuld, L. (2006). p. 57.

[34] Low, J. and P. C. Kalafut. (2002). *The Invisible Advantage: How Intangibles Are Driving Business Performance*. New York: Perseus Books. p. 79.

[35] For an interesting examination of Polaroid's response to the rise of digital imaging technology, see Tripsas, M. and G. Gavetti. "Capabilities, Cognition and Inertia: Evidence from Digital Imaging." *Strategic Management Journal*. 21: 1147–1161.

[36] The story of Pentagram's development of what became the Fuego line of high-end barbeque grills is chronicled in a Discovery Channel documentary titled "The Launch: A Product Is Born." It aired in April 2004, and it is now available for instructors to purchase. Faculty members may find it very useful when teaching about creativity, innovation, and new-product development. You might want to use it as a comparison case vis-à-vis the ABC News video of IDEO designing a new supermarket shopping cart. Students can examine the similarities and differences between the two firms' approaches.

[37] Ericsson, K. A., R. Krampe, and C. Tesch-Romer. (1993). "The role of deliberate practice in the acquisition of expert performance." *Psychological Review*. 100(3): 363–406.

[38] Ericsson, K. A., R. Krampe, and C. Tesch-Romer. (1993). p. 363.

[39] Ericsson, K. A., M. Prietula, and E. Cokely. (2007). "The making of an expert." *Harvard Business Review*. July–August: p. 114–121. The quote is on page 115.

[40] Ericsson, K. A., R. Krampe, and C. Tesch-Romer. (1993).

[41] Colvin, G. "What it takes to be great." *Fortune*. October 30, 2006.

[42] Ericsson, K. A., M. Prietula, and E. Cokely. (2007). p. 116.

[43] Bird, L. and B. Ryan. (1990). *Drive: The Story of My Life*. New York: Bantam. Sports fans, particularly Bostonians, will remember another remarkable left-handed shot that Bird made in a crucial playoff game. In Game 7 of the 1988 Eastern Conference Semifinals, the Celtics squared off against the Atlanta Hawks. In the fourth quarter of that game, Bird and Dominique Wilkins went toe-to-toe in a remarkable scoring duel. At one point, Bird drove into a crowd and hit an unbelievable left-handed scoop shot while being fouled. He finished the three-point play, of course! Bird scored twenty points in total during that quarter, and the Celtics prevailed.

[44] Williams, P. "Vic Braden's mental mojo experience." *New York Times*. October 29, 2006.

[45] Colvin, G. (2006).

[46] Ericsson, K. A., M. Prietula, and E. Cokely. (2007). p. 117.

[47] http://www.reuters.com/article/pressRelease/idUS77640+28-Jan-2008+BW20080128.

[48] Hira, N. "The making of a UPS driver." *Fortune*. November 12, 2007.

[49] http://www.pro-football-reference.com/.

9

The Mindset of a Problem-Finder

"In the beginner's mind there are many possibilities, but in the expert's there are few."
—Shunryu Suzuki, Japanese Zen priest

On July 17, 1981, roughly two thousand people attended a dance party at Kansas City's Hyatt Regency Hotel. Shortly after seven o'clock that evening, two overhead walkways collapsed onto the packed atrium below, killing one hundred fourteen people and injuring many others. The higher walkway gave way first, causing it to crash onto the lower walkway. Both structures then crashed onto the crowded atrium lobby below. Panic ensued throughout the hotel. A joyful dance party turned into a horrifying tragedy in a matter of seconds.[1]

An investigation revealed that a design modification had been made in the winter of 1979 during construction of the hotel. The change occurred to facilitate the construction process. However, the alteration in the design doubled the load on the hanger rod connections that were instrumental in supporting the walkways. The design no longer met the requirements of the Kansas City Building Code, yet the construction incorporated this flawed modification. After the collapse, many engineers lost their licenses due to complaints of negligence and misconduct filed by the Missouri Board of Architects, Professional Engineers, and Land Surveyors. Victims and their families received more than $100 million from legal settlements and judgments.

As it turned out, some problems had emerged during the construction of the hotel, but they were not investigated thoroughly. People did not recognize the potential warning signs. For instance, in October 1979, a large section of the atrium roof collapsed because of a problem with the roof connections. People examined the roof design and construction at that time, but they did not revisit the walkway design. Another signal of possible trouble emerged as workers transported materials and supplies across the walkways during the final stages of the project. Some employees complained that the walkways swayed and vibrated at times, particularly when full, heavy wheelbarrows were moved across them. Construction managers dismissed the workers' concerns; they did not examine whether a problem existed with the supporting structures. Instead, managers told the employees to take another route with the loaded wheelbarrows, thereby bypassing the walkways that traversed the atrium.

Now, consider a very different case in the field of structural engineering. William LeMessurier recounted this famous story to me in an interview conducted just a short time before his death in July 2007.[2] LeMessurier, a highly respected structural engineer, worked on the design of the Citicorp building at 53rd Street and Lexington Avenue in Manhattan. When completed in 1977, the skyscraper became the seventh-tallest building in the world. Then, in June 1978 a New Jersey engineering student placed a call to LeMessurier. Assigned by his professor to write a paper about the Citicorp building, the student quizzed LeMessurier about the four columns that supported the skyscraper. The young man's professor thought that the structural engineer had made a mistake. Why had he placed the columns in the middle of each side of the building, rather than at the corners? LeMessurier explained that the professor was incorrect and described why circumstances required the columns to be placed in the middle of each side. Moreover, he told the student about the unusual system of wind braces that he had invented for this building.

LeMessurier explained how the braces protected against the force of both perpendicular and quartering winds.[3]

After the conversation, LeMessurier thought about lecturing his own students at Harvard's Graduate School of Design on the topic of his unusual system of wind braces. When he designed the columns, he had calculated whether the building could resist perpendicular winds, as required by the New York City Building Code. The code did not require any calculations pertaining to quartering winds (that is, those approaching the building diagonally), and the engineering literature generally did not concern itself with the impact of quartering winds on rectangular buildings. However, this engineering student had sparked LeMessurier's curiosity. He decided to run a series of calculations pertaining to quartering winds. The results showed more strain on the braces than he expected. The finding proved rather unsettling.

LeMessurier then recalled a discovery he had made just a few weeks earlier. During a meeting to analyze plans for two buildings in Pittsburgh, a contractor asked a question about the welded joints called for in the design of wind braces similar to those used on the Citicorp building. LeMessurier called his New York office to ask about the construction of the welded joints. His office explained that contractors actually had used bolted joints on the Citicorp building; Bethlehem Steel had objected to the welded joints. In that firm's opinion, the building did not require the extra strength required by the welded joints, and bolts saved a substantial amount of money. LeMessurier's New York office had agreed to the change, and they had informed him. The office's decision seemed to make sense at the time, because the engineers considered only the perpendicular winds, as required by the New York City Building Code.

With his new calculations, LeMessurier wondered whether the bolted joints could withstand the stress of high quartering winds. In our interview, LeMessurier told me that his instincts suggested that a serious problem might exist. He felt compelled to investigate further.

He began to worry about a powerful storm triggering a catastrophic collapse of the building. He flew to Canada to speak with experts at the University of Western Ontario. He demanded a brutally honest assessment. They gave him one: the stress from quartering winds might exceed LeMessurier's latest calculations. He knew that he had a serious problem.

To his credit, LeMessurier took personal responsibility for the mistakes. He informed the building's architect and then flew to New York for a meeting with John Reed, then executive vice president of Citicorp (and later its Chairman and CEO). LeMessurier outlined the problem and then explained his strategy for repairing the building without alarming the public. Later, he met with Walter Wriston, Citicorp's Chairman. Repairs commenced soon after these meetings. LeMessurier recalled that both men treated him remarkably well throughout the process, and they did not try to punish him harshly for the errors. Over time, LeMessurier became an exalted figure in the field of structural engineering. People commended him for his willingness to be so forthcoming when he detected a potential flaw in his design.[4]

These two stories provide a stark contrast in the handling of information suggesting that a potential problem exists. The managers in the Kansas City hotel case dismissed the concerns of others and reaffirmed their belief in prior judgments by experts. Who were these construction workers to suggest that engineering experts might have made an error? William LeMessurier approached his situation with far more intellectual curiosity. Intrigued by the questions posed by a young engineering student far less knowledgeable than he, LeMessurier chose to perform additional analysis. In time, he began to question his earlier assumptions and judgments. He chose to pursue his concerns and obtain the perspective of unbiased experts. LeMessurier represents the quintessential problem-finder. He did not simply assume that his expert judgments were correct. When he detected trouble, he dug deeper. He wanted to understand the nature of the potential problem. He did not seek to assign blame to others, nor did he let the possibility of a disturbing answer suppress his investigation. LeMessurier clearly approached his situation with a very different mindset than the people involved in the Kansas City hotel tragedy.

Three Dimensions of a New Mindset

This book has argued that leaders at all levels must develop their problem-finding skills. We have provided an in-depth description of the seven critical skills and capabilities required to ensure that problems do not remain hidden in your organization. These processes and techniques will help you discover the bad news that typically does not surface until far too late. Becoming an effective problem-finder requires a different mindset, though, not simply a set of new behaviors and competencies. That mindset begins with a certain level of intellectual curiosity. You must be willing to ask questions, seeking always to learn more about both the familiar and the unfamiliar.

Intellectual Curiosity

Problem-finding requires a certain amount of intellectual curiosity. You must have a restless mind, one that is never satisfied with its understanding of a topic—no matter how much expertise and experience you have accumulated on the subject. You must have the instinct to explore puzzling questions that may challenge the conventional wisdom. You have to resist deferring to the experts who may feel that a particular matter is closed, that the knowledge base on that subject is complete and certain. Perhaps most importantly, you must be willing to question your own prior judgments and conclusions. That last point may be particularly troublesome for most of us. In her seminal study of how the U.S. government discounted warning signs prior to the Pearl Harbor attacks, Roberta Wohlstetter argued that human beings tend to exhibit a "stubborn attachment to existing beliefs."[5] Over the years, cognitive psychologists have provided ample evidence to support her contention. Effective problem-finders fight constantly against this urge to remain attached to prior beliefs. They exhibit a curiosity that causes them to question what others see as "set in stone."

The intellectually curious seek constantly to learn new things. They thrive on novelty. They seek out new situations and new ideas. Often, they find that these new experiences provide them a new perspective on the very familiar territory in which they work on a day-to-day basis. New research actually suggests that novelty stimulates the brain and enhances learning. For instance, in 2006, researchers at the University College of London conducted a study in which they showed subjects images of various scenes and faces while analyzing their brain activity using sophisticated scan technology. They discovered that new images stimulated the brain more than familiar ones, even if the familiar images were emotionally negative (such as an automobile accident or a face that appeared angry). In another set of experiments, the researchers tested the memory of subjects with regard to a set of novel images as well as more familiar ones. They discovered that subjects remembered more when new facts were mixed with more familiar data, as opposed to when individuals tried to memorize only common, recognizable information.[6]

Emory University professors Roderick Gilkey and Clint Kilts have argued that seeking novel experiences helps keep the brain sharp. They explain: "The more things you learn, the better you become at learning. Actively engaging in novel, challenging activities capitalizes on your capacity for neuroplasticity—the ability of your brain to reorganize itself adaptively and enhance its performance."[7] Problem-finding requires an ability to cope with ambiguity and to sort through seemingly contradictory signals at times. It requires a capacity to make sense of messy situations and a willingness to look at familiar situations from a different perspective. Novel learning experiences often provide us new conceptual models of how to think about a familiar situation as well as new frames of reference. Novel experience can shake our entrenched assumptions. A curious mind that enjoys learning new things may be a problem-finder's most valuable asset.[8]

Systemic Thinking

Successful problem-finders not only exhibit a curious mindset, but they also embrace systemic thinking. They recognize that small problems often do not occur due to the negligence or misconduct of an individual. Instead, small errors frequently serve as indicators of broader systemic issues in the organization. Effective problem-finders do not rush to find fault and assign blame when they spot a mistake being made. They step back and question why that error occurred. They ask whether more fundamental organizational problems have created the conditions that make that small error more likely to occur. Effective problem-finders recognize that you might fire the person who made an error on the front lines, but if you do not address the underlying systemic issues, the same errors will occur again and again. Firing someone who made a mistake without identifying the systemic problem does not constitute effective problem-finding; it simply means that you have found a convenient scapegoat.

Retired Brigadier General Duane Deal has an interesting perspective on the need for more systemic thinking among leaders. General Deal has studied a number of catastrophic failures. He has been a member of more than ten aircraft and space launch accident investigations, and he served on the *Columbia* Accident Investigation Board after the 2003 space shuttle accident.[9] General Deal recognizes that most complex failures do not have a single cause. Many small errors and mistakes often converge to create a catastrophe. Extensive scholarly research supports his contention. General Deal argues that we must resist the temptation to stop when we have spotted the most visible problem that may be causing trouble for the organization. To be an effective problem-finder, we have to dig deeper. What's behind that obvious problem? If it's a technical issue, we should ask: Why did this technical error occur? What organizational conditions and leadership failings may have contributed to the emergence and persistence of this technical problem? Deal argues that we must go "beyond the widget" when searching for the causes of major failures in our organizations:

> "Rarely is there a mishap caused by a single event or a broken widget. Therefore, after major mishaps—such as aviation and naval accidents—senior leaders must use that opportunity to look at the 'whole' organization. Even if the apparent cause of a flight accident is a broken part or an obvious pilot error, there are usually several other contributing factors."[10]

Healthy Paranoia

Andy Grove, former Chairman and CEO of Intel, once wrote a book titled *Only the Paranoid Survive*. In the preface, he described himself as quite a worrier. He said that he worried about everything from manufacturing problems to competitive threats to the failure to attract and retain the best talent. Many concerns kept him up at night. Grove argued that he believed fervently in the "value of paranoia."[11] He felt that leaders must never allow themselves to get comfortable, no matter how successful they had become. They had to devise ways of staying in touch with those in the organization who were willing to challenge the conventional wisdom, and who might alert them to bad news.

During my research for this book, I interviewed Kevin Walsh, the Chief Financial Officer of Hill Holliday, one of the nation's most successful advertising agencies.[12] Walsh had worked in a range of industries prior to arriving at the firm. Most recently, he had helped recharge growth and profitability at Zildjian, the historic cymbal company. Walsh has seen many companies go through deep troughs during his career, and he knows that many executives do not spot trouble until substantial damage has been done. At that point, the problems have become unwieldy, and the solutions have proven to be rather painful. By the time of problem recognition, perhaps the firm has entered a downward spiral that cannot be reversed. When Walsh came on board at Hill Holliday, he received words of advice from agency founder Jack Connors: "In our business, you have to remember that everything's rented, including us. You need to always be watching the front door because something is invariably slipping out the back door." Walsh always remembers those words. All leaders should adopt the mindset exemplified by this simple statement.

Effective problem-finders acknowledge that every organization, no matter how successful, has plenty of problems. They often lie beneath the surface, hidden from view. Effective problem-finders acknowledge their personal fallibility, rather than cultivating an aura of invincibility. They exhibit a healthy dose of paranoia, much like Andy Grove and Jack Connors. As noted psychiatrist Theodore Rubin once said, "The problem is not that there are problems. The problem is expecting otherwise and thinking that having problems is a problem."

Successful leaders demonstrate intellectual curiosity, adopt systemic thinking, and exhibit a healthy dose of paranoia. They do not wait for problems to come to them. They behave much more proactively. They seek out problems. They embrace them. You do not discover problems by sitting in your office waiting for the bad news to arrive at your door. The very best leaders know that speed is critical. The earlier you discover a problem, the more likely you can contain the damage, and the more likely you can solve it readily. Most importantly of all, successful leaders do not see problems as threats. They see every problem as an opportunity to learn and improve.

Endnotes

[1] This account of the Kansas City Hyatt walkways collapse draws on several sources: http://ethics.tamu.edu/ethics/hyatt/hyatt1.htm; Petroski, H. (1982). *To Engineer Is Human: The Role of Failure in Successful Design*. New York: Vintage Books.; Bruner, R. (2005). *Deals from Hell: M&A Lessons That Rise Above the Ashes*. Hoboken, NJ: John Wiley & Sons; http://antoine.frostburg.edu/phys/invention/case_studies/disasters/kansas_city_walkway.html.

[2] I am grateful to Bill Lovallo, a principal at LeMessurier Consultants, who put me in touch with William LeMessurier and vouched for me when I requested an interview. Mr. LeMessurier was kind enough to spend more than an hour with me on the phone from his home in Maine.

[3] This account draws from my interview with Mr. LeMessurier, as well as from an article written about the incident in the mid-1990s. Morgenstern, J. "The fifty-nine story crisis." *The New Yorker*. May 29, 1995. pp. 45–53. Gary Klein also provides an account in his book. Klein, G. (2004). *The Power of Intuition: How to Use Your Gut Feelings to Make Better Decisions at Work*. New York: Doubleday.

[4] When Mr. LeMessurier died in June 2007, his obituaries in the *New York Times* and the *Boston Globe* discussed this incident at length and commended him for his willingness to be forthcoming about the design flaw.

[5] Wohlstetter, R. (1962). *Pearl Harbor: Warning and Decision*. Stanford, CA: Stanford University Press. p. 393.

[6] Fenker, D., J. Frey, H. Schuetze, D. Heipertz, H-J Heinze, and E. Duzel. (2008). "Novel scenes improve recollection and recall of words." *Journal of Cognitive Neuroscience*. 20(7): 1250–1265.

[7] Gilkey, R. and C. Kilts. (2007). "Cognitive fitness." *Harvard Business Review*. November: 53–66.

[8] Gary Hamel also often advocates that executives should seek out novelty as a means of stimulating creativity and innovation in their organizations. See Hamel, G. and L. Välikangas. (2003). "The quest for resilience." *Harvard Business Review*. September: 52–63.

[9] I came to know Retired General Duane Deal when I was studying the *Columbia* space shuttle accident. He graciously agreed to come to my class to speak to my students when I taught the multimedia case to MBAs for the first time. General Deal gave a magnificent talk to the students, and I was able to speak with him at length about his perspective on the causes of catastrophic failures. I met up with General Deal again when I was presenting my research at the Johns Hopkins Applied Physics Laboratory, where he went to work after retiring from the U.S. Air Force.

[10] Deal, D. W. (2004). "Beyond the widget: Columbia accident lessons affirmed." *Air and Space Power Journal*. Summer: 31–50.

[11] Grove, A. (1999). *Only the Paranoid Survive*. New York: Currency/Doubleday. p. 3.

[12] Interview with Kevin Walsh in his office at Hill Holliday in Boston, Massachusetts. Mr. Walsh agreed initially to a one-hour interview, but he ended up spending almost an entire morning with me. I am very grateful to him for being so generous with his time.

INDEX